Precious Paper Dolls

by Cynthia Erfurt Musser
in collaboration with Joyce D. McClelland

Published by 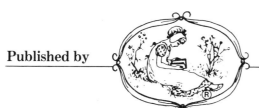 Hobby House Press, Inc.
Cumberland, Maryland 21502

Dedication

To our husbands, Phil and Les, for their continued support and understanding.

Acknowledgements

I am most appreciative of the friendships of all of the doll and paper doll collectors who have in their own ways shared with me their knowledge and pleasure in collecting. It was my desire, in return, to share with these friends that inspired me to compile this book.

My special thanks to Joyce McClelland for her inspiration, encouragement and support throughout the writing of this book, for the use of her extensive collection and for her knowledgeable counsel.

My gratitude to my good friend, Patti Fertel, who was constantly helpful in so many ways.

Sincere thanks to Zelda Cushner, Louise Kaufman, Maurine Popp, Richard Rusnock, Janie and Emalee Varsolona and Judith Whorton for their special contributions and advice.

I am grateful to the following people for sharing their paper dolls, time and knowledge in compiling this book: Janie Barrett, Virginia Crossley, Agnes Durcholz, Jennie Edgar, Rosalie Eppert, Barbara Ferguson, Patricia Foster, Marie Hajma, Shirley Hedge, Pam Hunter, Barbara Jendrick, Genie Kalb, Joan Carol Kaltschmidt, Elizabeth Landis, Louise Leek, Edith Linn, Elizabeth McIntyre, Katharine McIntyre, Ted Menten, Grayce Piemontesi, Peggy Jo Rosamond, Phyllis Salak, Pat Stall, Jane Sugg, Suzanne Tessey, Paige Thornton, Anne Wallach, Jean Woodcock and Mary Young.

Special thanks to my mother who introduced me to dolls and paper dolls and to my aunts, Virginia, Marthalee and Maxie, who spent many hours playing paper dolls with me as a child.

WHICH WILL YOU HAVE?

REMIT IN MONEY ORDER, POSTAL NOTE OR STAMPS.

from *Doll's Dressmaker*, January 1891.

Unless otherwise noted, all paper dolls are from the collection of Cynthia E. Musser and all photographs were taken by her.

Additional copies of this book may be purchased at $14.95
plus $1.75 postage/handling from
Hobby House Press, Inc.
900 Frederick Street, Cumberland, Maryland 21502

CONTENTS

Brides, Brides, Brides 2
Victorian Ladies and Gents 15
Victorian Children 53
Elegant Edwardians 74
Children of the Teens and Twenties 85
Favorite Families 130
Bears and Such 151
Two Talented Sisters -- Drayton and Hays 167
Kewpies Forever 192
Brownies, Delightful Brownies 210
Celebrated Royalty 221

Introduction

Paper dolls have given great pleasure to children and adults for over 100 years. These fragile, flat figures have much knowledge to share — about children, parents' attitudes about children, personalities, economies of the times and current styles.

While it is possible to collect paper dolls and enjoy them just for their celebrated faces or their delightful, childlike appearances, when these "Precious Paper Dolls" are viewed in a historical perspective, they reveal another whole dimension to collecting.

This book clusters paper dolls and paper toys by themes, to discuss and illustrate the social and historical forces that these paper treasures record and reflect. Hopefully, the next time you study your own collection, you will view it with new enthusiasm

and insight. Perhaps you will also be encouraged to begin to add to your collection some paper dolls to enhance the themes that — consciously or unconsciously — have been developing.

This book is intended to be a historical and pictorial reference to paper dolls and paper toys. Throughout there has been a great effort to achieve completeness and accuracy. The information concerning period fashion trends should also be helpful in dating unidentified paper dolls.

Other nostalgia and emphemera collectors may also find this book helpful to them for its historical information.

Enjoy!

Brides, Brides, Brides, . . .

Chapter 1

Being a bride has, for generations, been one of the most joyous moments in a lifetime. Steeped in tradition, filled with romantic ideals and encircled with the blessings of society, it has been the culmination of a young woman's dreams. It has been the moment little girls were raised to wish for. The bride's gown, even today, is often the most beautiful and elaborate one she may ever own. It is no wonder that the bride has become the subject of many special sets of paper dolls. These bridal sets range from those focusing on the bride and her trousseau alone to those with the full wedding party, and even some including the family of the bride and groom as well as some of the wedding guests.

These bridal sets, for the most part, are a marvelous record of many of the styles that form modern bridal tradition. In earlier times, the bridal gowns were very much influenced by the styles worn by royalty. Queen Victoria set the fashion trends during the early part of her reign, and when she married wore a full skirted gown with wide flounces and a low, off the shoulder neckline. When Napoleon III married Eugenie de Montijo, a Spanish countess, it had a great impact on the fashion world and the styling of her magnificent gown was often copied with its wide skirt trimmed in broad flounces of lace, its close fitting bodice, long sleeves and long veil.

In 1878, the wedding of Queen Victoria's eldest daughter, the Princess Royale, caught the eye of the world. Her gown was designed by Charles Frederick Worth. For the occasion he chose a close fitting style with no waistline which has come to be known as the "princess style." Worth designed wedding gowns for all of the elite of Europe and his styles have had a lasting impact on bridal fashions that carries over into current styling. He adopted the court train for brides, some of which were from 4yds (3.64m) to 7yds (6.37m) long! It was he who first used the long, sweeping wedding veil. He worked in rich satin, bouffant tulle and wide silk ribbon. He decorated his gowns with ribbon in bows and streamers.

Bridal fashions have reflected the styles of each period, but within the boundaries of wedding tradition. Early wedding gowns were not always white. The brides often wore pastels. They chose rich, heavy silks and added whatever lace they possessed. Lace was so valuable it was measured by the inch, never cut, and many gowns had several different patterns

decorating them. The wedding gown then became the bride's best dress and was often worn to go calling because the bride was expected to visit each wedding guest within the first year of her marriage. White first began to be used as a color for wedding gowns around 1820 when fashion turned to the classic Greek and Roman styling for inspiration.

The orange blossom became the bride's flower, but many girls chose to carry a fan or bible rather than flowers. The fan was often a gift from the groom and made of precious materials — sometimes jewel trimmed — of great value.

The journey to a new home dictated the need for a going-away dress and by the 1850s a lavish trousseau was a necessity. This wardrobe was paid for by the bride's father and became a show of his wealth. The bride-to-be spent some time monogramming the personal items of her trousseau in her finest needlework.

By the 1890s, wedding gowns with full skirts over crinoline petticoats and styles with bustles had disappeared and the brides chose gowns with gored skirts and wide sleeves. This style soon gave way to the Gibson Girl look.

The bridal paper dolls that were produced always followed the trends of the current fashion. In the mid 1870s the McLoughlin Brothers Printing Company produced the "Paper Doll Bridal Party" in three folder booklets — *The Bride*, the *Bridesmaid* and the *Bridegroom and Groomsman*. Each booklet sold for fifteen cents. In this beautiful early series the bride has a pink wedding gown trimmed with ribbons and ruching and yards of lace. The gown has a bustle in back flowing into a train and a floor length veil. She wears the traditional orange blossoms in her hair. Her three other gowns and matching accessories are very typical of 1870s fashion and each one is lavish. The groom and groomsman come in one folder together. The men dolls, unlike the ladies who appear in their underwear, are already attired in their tails for the wedding. Four other costumes fit interchangeably over the dressed gentlemen. Each of the men's garments is fashionably correct to the dictates of the period.

Another wonderful bride is believed to have been printed in Germany, first, and later reproduced by the McLoughlin Brothers. Information is not conclusive but some think that she may be Empress

Alexandra Feodorovna (Princess Dagmar of Denmark, sister to Alexandra, wife of Edward VII of England). The early paper doll and her clothes are deeply embossed, printed in rich color, front and back. She measures 6⅛in (15.5cm). The later paper dolls, which came in two sizes, are entitled, *Diane, the Bride*. They are lithographed but not embossed. One of these dolls measures 4in (10.2cm); the other, 6⅝in (16.8cm).

The Raphael Tuck Company, well known for their lavish and wonderful paper dolls, produced *Our Little Treasure* which shows the different stages of a woman's life and, of course, includes a lovely wedding gown. The floor length veil is trimmed in orange blossoms, the bodice decorated in lace and the fabric of the gown looks as if it is the richest white satin. One of the most sought after Tuck series today is the "Bridal Series of Dressing Dolls." It is made up of four separately boxed paper dolls — the *Bride*, the *Bridegroom*, the *Maid of Honor* and the *Bridesmaid*. In addition to the bridal costumes, each has three other die-cut costumes for, perhaps, taking part in prebridal festivities. These paper dolls are printed on heavy cardboard with the Tuck patented heads. The *Bride*, *Bridegroom* and *Bridesmaid* have also been found produced on heavy weight paper in sheets to be cut out. These sheets were part of large boxed sets with a number of sheets of various paper dolls included. The members of the wedding party produced in sheet form are unmarked when cut out but the dolls and their costumes are identical to the more deluxe die-cut sets except only three costumes were printed on the sheets.

Companies that wanted to use paper dolls to advertise their products quickly produced bridal sets knowing that they would be popular with the little girls. The McLaughlin's Coffee Company advertised a series of 16 ladies — one lady with an extra costume in each pound of coffee. This series includes several beautiful brides. The Singer Sewing Machine Company offered a bride wearing the latest Gibson Girl fashions. The gowns were from patterns available from the Economy Pattern Company. Ayers Sarsparilla and Pectoral Medicine extolled the benefits of their products with yet another paper doll bride. This one was drawn with the childlike face and called *Doll Bride* to resemble a bisque doll. Cleverly the pieces are reversible, giving the bride four costumes. The advertising which appears on the flap of the dress assures:

> Children like it. It is quick to act and
> sure to cure and should be in every
> house in which there are boys and
> girls.

The doll was available for 12 cents in stamps. Clark's ONT Spool Cotton offered a complete wedding party with 12 figures which they called the "Dolls' Wedding Series." It also came through the mail in exchange for three 2 cent stamps. Sometime later the company

offered a second set, but this one had only seven dolls, again in exchange for six cents in stamps.

It was not until 1909 that the bridal party was introduced in American magazines. The "Lettie Lane" series in *The Ladies' Home Journal* began one of the largest and most beautiful wedding parties ever produced. The bride, the groom, the wedding party and guests were all lavishly dressed in the most handsome Edwardian fashions.

These pages must have been very popular, for today many of these paper dolls, cut and uncut, continue to turn up having been tucked away all these years, too precious to discard. *The Ladies' Home Journal* began another series in 1915 with *Lettie Lane* introducing *Betty Bonnet*. Both the *Lettie Lane* and the *Betty Bonnet* pages were drawn by artist Sheila Young. By 1918, this series also pub-

Illustration 1. Betty Bonnet Goes to a Wedding, from The Ladies' Home Journal, June 1918.

lished bride and groom pages. But this time fashion dictated more simple styles and the costumes definitely reflected the attitudes of the war years.

Other magazines offering paper dolls also used the bridal theme. Under the influence of the war years, in 1918, *The Delineator* printed a cut-out series drawn by Corwin Knapp Linson which included *Tommy Atkins on Furlough*, depicting a young soldier on leave from the army to marry his bride. *McCall's, Pictorial Review, Good Housekeeping, Ladies' World* and *Woman's Home Companion* all eventually printed pages featuring paper dolls as brides.

The blushing bride seems to have a special and lasting charm as these beautiful brides are still, today, some of the paper dolls most sought after by collectors.

McLOUGHLIN BROTHERS' PAPER DOLL BRIDAL PARTY.

LEFT: Illustration 2. 7⅞in (20cm) *The Bride*, a paper doll with its envelope front published in booklet form circa 1875, which originally sold for 15 cents.

BELOW LEFT: Illustration 3. Uncut page of clothes from *The Bride*.

BELOW RIGHT: Illustration 4. Uncut page of clothes from *The Bride*.

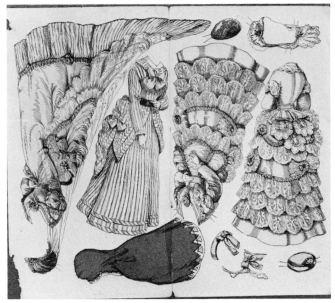

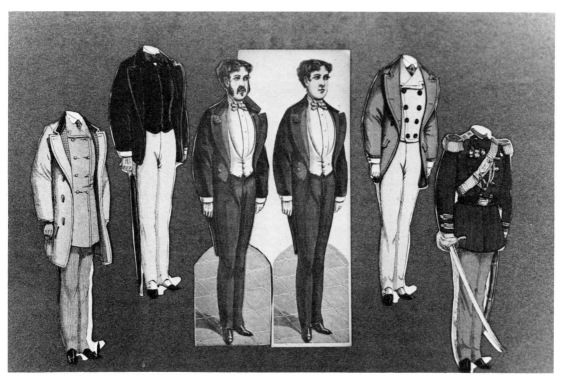

ABOVE: *Illustration 5.* 8½in (21.6cm) *Bridegroom and Groomsman.* Two dolls and four outfits which are interchangeable. (Hats are not shown.)

BELOW LEFT: *Illustration 6.* Envelope from *Bridegroom and Groomsman.*

BELOW RIGHT: *Illustration 7.* 6⅛in (15.5cm) German embossed bride dating from the 1880s. She was later reproduced in the 4in (10.2cm) and 6⅝in (16.8cm) sizes as *Diane, the Bride* by McLoughlin Brothers.

THE BRIDAL SERIES OF DRESSING DOLLS
BY RAPHAEL TUCK

This series is outstanding for its lifelike artwork and subtle watercolor effects. It was printed as four individually boxed, die-cut sets; and the bride, bridegroom and bridesmaid also appeared printed on thinner sheets to be cut out as part of *Father Tuck's Doll Sheets*. All of the die-cut paper dolls in this series are marked "By Special Appointment Publishers To Her Majesty The Queen, Raphael Tuck and Sons, Ltd., London, Paris, New York."

Illustration 8. 9½in (24.2cm) No. 1 *The Bride and Her Trousseau,* Artistic Series 600, the "Bridal Party Series of Dressing Dolls" includes costume A, the bridal gown and veil; costume B, a yellow gown with a pink feather boa; the bride, costume C, a blue walking suit with a striped blouse; and costume D, a red jacket and green plaid skirt for golfing.

Illustration 9. The Bridal Party — *Bridesmaid, Bridegroom, Bride* and *Maid of Honor* — in their wedding attire. *McClelland Collection.*

Illustration 10. 9½in (24.2cm) No. 2 *The Bridegroom with Suits and Hats,* Artistic Series 601, the "Bridal Party Series of Dressing Dolls" includes costume A, the groom's formal attire; costume B, a tan jacket over blue striped trousers with a white shirt and ascot with tan bowler; the groom, costume C, a military uniform (notice US on the belt buckle); and costume D, a brown lounging jacket, pink striped shirt and green plaid pants with matching hat.

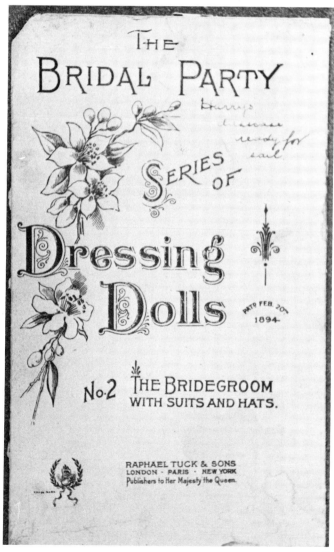

Illustration 11. Box lid for *The Bridegroom with Suits and Hats. McClelland Collection.*

ABOVE: Illustration 12. 9½in (24.2cm) No. 3 The Maid of Honor, Her Gowns and Hats, Artistic Series 602, the "Bridal Party Series of Dressing Dolls" includes costume A, a dress of blue polka dots on white with other blue trim; costume B, for the wedding, a cream colored gown trimmed with yellow ribbons and pink roses; the maid of honor, costume C, a walking suit in green with a pink and white inset bodice and front; and costume D, a tan jacket over a yellow skirt. *McClelland Collection.*

BELOW: Illustration 13. 9½in (24.2cm) No. 4 The Bridesmaid with Complete Outing Costumes, Artistic Series 603, the "Bridal Party Series of Dressing Dolls" includes costume A, for the wedding, a cream colored gown trimmed with blue ribbons and violets; costume B, a walking suit with a tan jacket and a black fur boa over a tan and aqua plaid skirt with a black and white spotted dog; the bridesmaid, costume C, a boating ensemble in blue and trimmed with red; and costume D, a cycling outfit in pale green with a red striped blouse and red and green plaid skirt.

ABOVE: *Illustration 14.* 5¾in (14.7cm) *Brides* published by the McLaughlin Coffee Company to help promote their coffee. Left, paper doll No. 1 and right, paper doll No. 4, both from the series of "sixteen ladies." Each set of the series includes one doll and four costume pieces. (The capes are not shown.)

BELOW: *Illustration 15.* 9in (22.9cm) *Singer Sewing Machine Bride,* (cut) offered to promote not only Singer Sewing Machines, but also Economy Patterns because all of the bride's costumes were available as patterns. On the left is the elegant wedding gown in white, next a stylish green walking suit with navy collar and cuffs and straw hat. The bride is dressed in a white slip trimmed with blue ribbons. The third gown is a blue and white check trimmed with a blue sash. The gown on the far right is white with blue dots. (Bride's veil and a straw hat trimmed in flowers are missing.) *McClelland Collection.*

ABOVE: Illustration 16. 9¾in (24.9cm) *Ayer's Doll Bride* was produced to advertise Ayer's patent medicine. The dresses and hats for this doll are reversible, showing four different costumes; the doll, which was copyrighted in 1895, was available for 12 cents in stamps.

BELOW: Illustration 17. Reverse side of the clothes for the *Ayer's Doll Bride.*

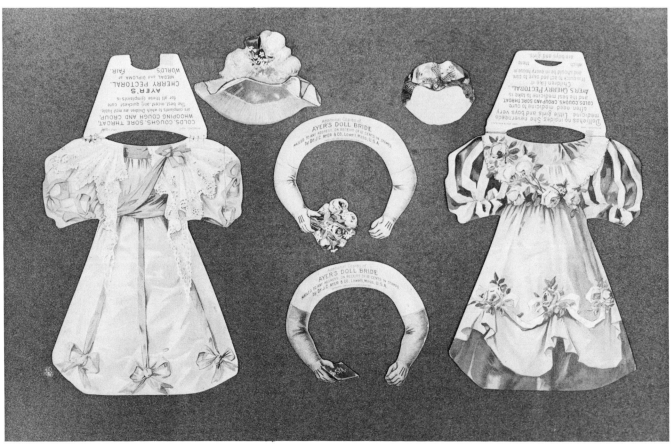

ABOVE: *Illustration 18.* Each measuring 5¼in (13.3cm) tall, the 12 dolls in Clark's ONT Thread *Dolls' Wedding Series* were offered as a set by sending three two-cent stamps to the company. Left to right: Top, *Best Man, Minister, Bridesmaid with Forget-Me-Nots, Bridesmaid with Pansies;* Middle, *Groom, Bride, Bridesmaid with Daisies, Father of the Bride;* Bottom, *Father of the Groom, Mother of the Groom, Bridesmaid with Roses, Mother of the Bride.* (Note, the bridesmaids should have the same flowers in their hair that they have in their bouquets. These two-piece dolls often become mixed.) *Some pieces Barrett Collection.*

BELOW: *Illustration 19.* Clark's ONT *Wedding Set,* from left to right: *Mother of the Bride,* the *Bridesmaid,* the *Bride,* the *Minister,* the *Groom,* the *Best Man* and the *Father of the Bride.* This complete set of seven dolls was available from the company for six cents in stamps. This set, influenced by World War I, appeared sometime after the "Dolls' Wedding Series." *McClelland Collection.*

Illustration 20. *Toy Sheet* printed by the Universal Toy Company, circa 1905. *McClelland Collection.*

Illustration 21. 7in (17.8cm) *Bride No. 0102,* cut from a sheet, published by McLoughlin Brothers after 1900. *McClelland Collection.*

OPPOSITE PAGE: Illustration 22. 12¾in (32.5cm) *Our Little Treasure* published by Raphael Tuck is a die-cut doll with six costumes and three known hats (one hat not pictured), showing the different stages in a woman's life. All of the pieces are heavily embossed and delicately colored. She has soft brown hair and brown eyes; her camisole is colored turquoise and her petticoat, white with turquoise trim. She is wearing brown shoes and stockings. Each of her six costumes exemplifies a stage of her life. Her wardrobe includes: A green sailor dress trimmed in rose with a matching tam; a light brown dress with a green bodice and hat of brown straw with plaid trim; a turquoise gown accented with ecru and a matching turquoise hat trimmed with a bow; an ivory wedding gown with a separate veil trimmed in flowers; a rose-colored formal gown with a feather fan; and, the traditional black dress for a woman in mourning. The back of the doll and her clothes are marked with the palette and easel, and "Art Publishers by Royal Warrant, Designed at the Studios in England and printed at the Fine Art Works in Saxony." *McClelland Collection.*

Illustration 23. Tommy Atkins on Furlough drawn by Corwin Knapp Linson for *The Delineator*, May 1918.

Illustration 24. Margery May's Big Sister designed by M. Emma Musselman for the *Woman's Home Companion*, June 1921.

Victorian Ladies and Gents

The Victorian age has provided us with some wonderful, rich and elaborate paper dolls and paper toys. The period itself, which was noted for lavish styles, rich fabrics and intricate designs to excess, spanned over 60 years. Men and women valued modesty, conformity and respectability. All of these aspects of Victorian life are reflected in the paper dolls and paper toys that were abundantly produced at that time.

The Victorians especially loved all kinds of paper goods and collected them into wonderful scrapbooks which they displayed in their parlors. Much of the early printing was done in Germany. The paper was of high quality and early paper dolls were hand colored. During this period books for the first time became readily available to children. As processes of printing improved, paper was often elegantly embossed and printing was soon in full, rich color. The abundance of paper goods was overwhelming. By the 1890s, all kinds of products were promoted with advertising cards, pamphlets and very popular paper dolls.

The Industrial Revolution had a great influence on the Victorian Age. During this time a new affluent middle class emerged. The rural, farm-based society shifted to an urban industrialized one. These people had never possessed title or position but through industralization had amassed great fortunes very quickly. This new class of people were anxious to display their new wealth.

During Victoria's reign the sewing machine was invented, leading the way for ready-made clothing and soon machines were turning out ready-made lace as well. Middle class ladies now wore the same clothes as the upper classes. By 1860, aniline dyes were being developed which made brighter colors possible. Many of the inventions that continue to be important today were being developed during the Victorian years — the incandescent electric light, the automobile and motion picture. During these years the early labor unions began to form.

It is not difficult to understand how all of these things affected fashion for men and women, and the paper dolls left to us from these years reflect the variety of styles that the Victorians chose to express their changing lifestyles.

In Europe before the 1850s some wonderful, boxed and gilded paper dolls were produced. Each garment was carefully hand colored. These treasured sets were sometimes exported to America.

The real beginning of paper dolls that would be easily available to larger numbers of children came during the 1850s in America when early printing companies like Brown, Taggard and Chase; Clark, Austin and Smith; and McLoughlin Brothers, who already produced children's books, began to produce penny and nickel paper dolls in envelope and booklet form.

Fashion lady paper dolls reflect the costumes of the era with wide skirts supported by crinolines and hoops. Examples such as Clark, Austin, and Smith's *Clara* and McLoughlin Brothers' *American Lady*, *Lady Gay* and *Little Lady* capture the feeling of daintiness and femininity of the clothing and the abundant use of laces. The hats and accessories were tiny and ladies generally wore only a short jacket or "fichu" as a wrap. Early in the period styles were very much influenced by Queen Victoria.

The silhouette of the young ladies' fashions was very much like that of their mothers with wide skirts emphasizing narrow waistlines and wide feminine necklines revealing shoulders and necks. Young ladies, however, wore their skirts shorter, permitting their legs to show and often dainty ruffled pantaloons were exposed. McLoughlin Brothers' paper dolls, *Ida Mae* and *Minnie Miller*, show the proper young ladies' attire and capture the elaborate detail of the costumes at that time.

The 1870s brought an entire change in the feminine silhouette as the bustle gained popularity. Prince Albert died in 1861 and Queen Victoria entered a period of mourning. With little royalty remaining in power in Europe, fashion began to take its cue from theatrical personalities. Still the richness and trimmings, so very Victorian, predominated. Fashion extravagance dictated that affluent women wear two skirts — the top one looped up and tied behind the waist, revealing a second plain underskirt beneath. Women favored heavier fabrics and dark rich colors. McLoughlin Brothers' paper doll, *Betsy Brunette*, from the "Dolly Varden" series and *Little Dolly Varden* from the "Little Dolly Varden" series well reflect this period. The term "Dolly Varden" originated with a popular character of the times from the Dicken's story "Barnaby Rudge." Dolly Varden was the daughter of a simple locksmith. She was quite flirtacious and loose with her admirers. Dolly dressed in the "Watteau" style which featured a full, flowing skirt and a tight bodice with a low neckline trimmed with ruffles and elbow length ruffled sleeves that was very appealing to the gentlemen. Her character had such an impact that by the mid seventies, "Dolly Varden" had become the popular name for a vari-colored shirtwaist with a bustle and hat imitated from Watteau. With some modifications, the bustle continued through the eighties.

In 1859, *Godey's Lady's Book* became the first to include paper dolls in their magazine. In 1866, *Frank Leslie's Magazine* printed a lovely lady with six dresses. A lesser known series entitled "La Poupee Modele" was published in a French magazine called *Journal des Petites Filles* during the late sixties and into the seventies. Information is sketchy but the lovely paper dolls are found printed front and back and are delicately colored.

Early in the Victorian period gentlemen adopted long trousers, and during the coming years the basic dark suit evolved. Trousers, which now buttoned down the front, were worn so long that they covered the heel of the shoe.

Gentlemen favored dark green, blue and black. The suit coat was referred to as a frock coat or a "Prince Albert." It was usually double-breasted and came to just above the knee. Shirts were generally white and pleated across the front. Fashionable trousers were not of the same material as the frock coats but were usually striped, checked or plain. Topcoats were referred to as "dustcoats" and gray was the favorite color. Suspenders held up knee-length socks and braces held up a gentleman's trousers. A gentleman's starched collar first stood up; later it was turned down.

The handsome unidentified gentleman, pictured, is richly colored and embossed and was surely made in Germany. His wardrobe is the epitome of Victorian fashion.

By the 1890s, all of the changes that society had experienced were beginning to modify fashion. The paper dolls of this decade reveal fashions for men and women that were more suitable to their current lifestyle. Some women began to venture out of the home to work while others began to participate in sports such as swimming, cycling and golf. Their clothing underwent drastic liberating changes. Corsets and bustles disappeared in favor of the natural waistline and emphasis shifted to the shoulders and sleeves. Skirts were raised completely off the ground.

For sports such as cycling women began to wear pants and most often adapted men's fashions for their most stylish costumes. In what has come to be known as the grassroots of the women's liberation movement, ladies gained new independence with the advent of cycling. For the first time a proper, young, single woman could go out unchaperoned. A whole new dimension in fashion developed — sports clothes. Suits with tailored jackets and short skirts with leggings or pants were popular. Bloomers, a short skirt over long, loose trousers that gathered in at the ankle, became fashionable. From them came "Turkish pants," "Zouave trousers," which were adapted from French infantry uniforms and naval reefer jackets. Women donned men's hats and caps to complete their cycling attire.

The Pope Manufacturing Company, maker of Columbia bicycles, produced a set of six paper dolls to promote their deluxe bicycles for women. On the inside flap the company goes into some detail to describe each of the smart cycling costumes by fashion designers of renown.

An unusual paper doll pair, *Lady Cyclists Up To Date*, came in an envelope marked "printed in Bavaria." The dolls are in rich color and deeply embossed. Each fashionably dressed lady slips off and on her bicycle. The bicycles have easel backs so that they can stand. Marked at "Threepence per packet" and "London," they were undoubtedly designed for the English trade.

At this time the newspapers were including special color supplements in their Sunday editions to help increase circulation. In 1895, *The Boston Sunday Herald* and a number of other newspapers began a series of fashion paper dolls that has come to be known as the "Boston Herald Ladies." The series includes two dolls and a wonderful wardrobe that grew over the weeks to include over 50 known costumes. Not all of the costumes appeared in all of the newspapers. Fashion was always important in these supplements. Generally, each plate also showed a sketch of the back of the garment. The newspapers offered the patterns for making these wonderful clothes.

In 1895, a family was published that remains a mystery. It is beautifully lithographed in full color and marked only "MC&K." Except for the grandparents who look like George and Martha Washington, the rest of the family are actually dressed in the style of the nineties.

Another interesting example from this period was a family produced by the C. I. Hood Company of Massachusetts to advertise its patent medicine. The family, which was copyrighted in 1894, consisted of father, mother, two daughters and a son. Each paper doll had two extra costumes and appropriate hats. The set totaled 19 pieces. The back of each doll and each costume was covered with advertising claims promoting cures for "disordered nerves, sleeplessness, weak blood, and disagreeable eruptions." As an added reminder, father and son each had packages of Hood's Sarsparilla peeping out of their pockets. After all, the company did not want anyone to forget, "there is no remedy equal to Hood's Sarsparilla." The set was originally obtained by sending in one trademark from Hood's Pills and ten cents in stamps to the company. A second set of Hood's paper dolls also turns up occasionally. The dolls are identical, but the clothing appears to have been redesigned to turn-of-the-century styles. Advertising materials found with this set of dolls suggest that they were available for only six one cent stamps!

The Victorians left a rich heritage for paper doll collectors to appreciate and enjoy.

DIE SCHWESTERN

Die Schwestern, "Two Sisters," is a rare and wonderful boxed set which was embossed and printed in deep, rich color in Germany circa 1895. The set includes a beautiful wardrobe and a number of accessories for each doll and a splendid dressing table. *McClelland Collection.*

RIGHT: Illustration 25. Die Schwestern — box lid.

Illustration 26. Die Schwestern, the younger sister.

Illustration 27. Die Schwestern, the older sister.

TWO CLARAS COMPARED

These two paper dolls are nearly identical and represent one of the questions that probably will never be fully explained. The dolls' bodies are identical; only their heads are different. Four of their five gowns are also the same. It appears that sometime after Clark, Austin, & Smith produced their *Clara*, McLoughlin Brothers got a hold of the design and made minor changes, perhaps to make the set more appealing. McLoughlin Brothers also produced other dolls which were similar to ones published by Clark, Austin, & Smith among them — *Hattie*, *Nellie North*, *The Little Pet* and *Cinderella*.

ABOVE: Illustration 28. 5¾in (14.7cm) *Clara* No. 5 from "The Little Girl's Delight" series published by Clark, Austin & Smith of New York, copyright 1857.

BELOW: Illustration 29. Clara published by Clark, Austin & Smith — clothes.

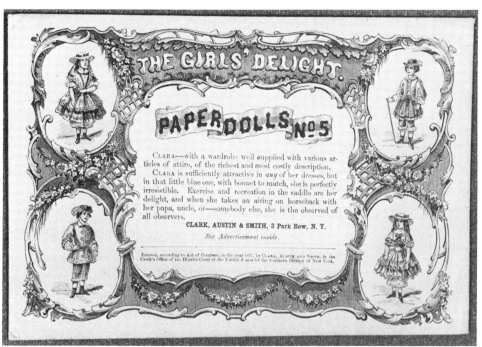

Illustration 30. Envelope for *Clara* by Clark, Austin & Smith.

Illustration 31. 5¾in (14.7cm) *Clara West* published by McLoughlin Brothers and advertised in their 1875 catalog. *Fertel Collection.*

Illustration 32. 6¼in (15.8cm) *The American Lady with Something to Wear,* No. 2, published by McLoughlin Brothers, copyright 1858. *McClelland Collection.*

Illustration 33. American Lady with Something to Wear — envelope. McClelland Collection.

Illustration 34. 7½in (19.1cm) *Lady Gay* published by McLoughlin Brothers and advertised in 1859 as a "beautiful doll, extra large." The doll and clothes are printed front and back. She originally came in an envelope with four costumes to be cut out.

Illustration 35. 5in (12.7cm) *Little Lady* is from the "Early Series" published by McLoughlin Brothers in 1858. This must have been a very popular set because it continued to be advertised in the 1870s. *Little Lady* originally sold for ten cents.

Illustration 36. 7¾in (19.8cm) *Ida Mae* was advertised by McLoughlin Brothers in 1858. She was an extra large doll, like *Lady Gay,* also printed front and back. She originally came in an envelope with four costumes to be cut out which sold for 20 cents.

Illustration 37. 3⅛in (7.9cm) *Minnie Miller* was advertised by McLoughlin Brothers in 1859. She is printed front only and came in an envelope with four costumes to be cut out which sold for five cents. Because of her small size, she has several mask faces showing her bonnets.

Illustration 38. 11in (27.9cm) *Betsy Brunette*, one of the "Dolly Varden Dolls," was advertised by the McLoughlin Brothers during the 1870s. She is brightly colored and printed front and back. These "Dolly Varden Dolls" are the largest paper dolls that McLoughlin Brothers ever made.

Illustration 39. Betsy Brunette — envelope.

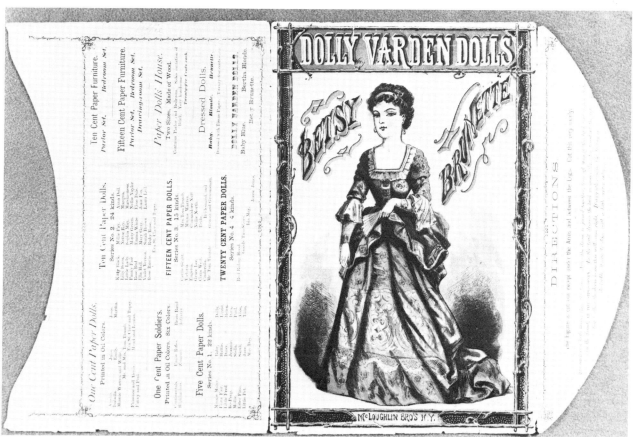

Illustration 40. 4in (10.2cm) *Little Dolly Varden* from the "Little Dolly Varden Series" is cut, but originally came uncut, in folder form, printed front only. These little folders sold for a penny in the 1870s. *McClelland Collection.*

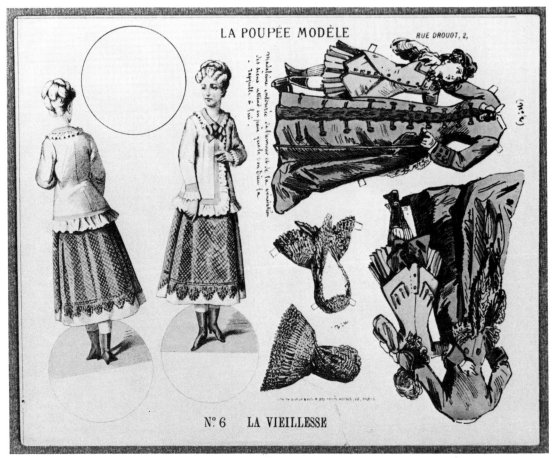

Illustration 41. "La Poupee Modele," No. 6 *La Vieillesse,* from the *Journal des Petite Filles,* is marked "lith. Th. Dupuy et Fils. Rue des Petite - Hotels 22 Paris." The doll has a round base which, according to Marian Howard, is very typical of French paper dolls.

Illustration 42. 6¼in (16.5cm) German embossed man is cut and unmarked, but has a stylish Victorian wardrobe.

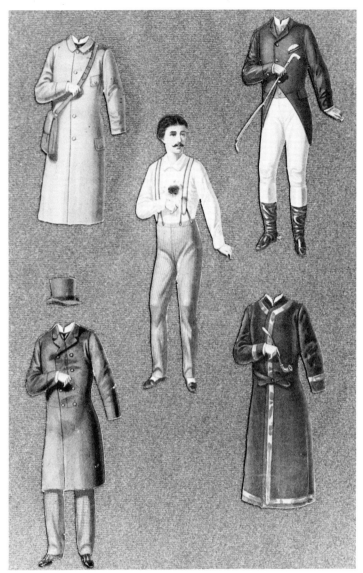

Illustration 43. 6½in (16.5cm) German embossed lady is cut and unmarked, but she is very similar to the German embossed bride found in chapter one and was also later reproduced by McLoughlin Brothers in a smaller size which was not embossed. *Fertel Collection.*

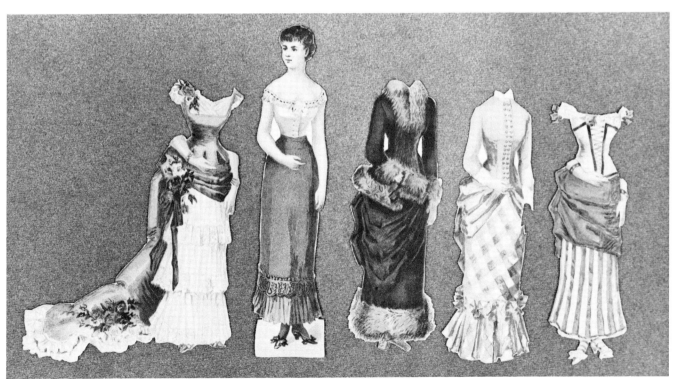

COLUMBIA BICYCLE LADIES

These ladies in their cycling attire were printed
by the Pope Manufacturing Company to promote
their deluxe Columbia bicycles. The set of six dolls
was mailed in exchange for five two-cent stamps.

Illustration 44. Costume designed by Redfern. "An extremely
smart costume, consisting of short skirt worn over knickerbockers of the same material, and waist with vest of red cloth
and gold buttons under front of light box cloth. Leggings of
box cloth. Alpine hat. The material recommended by Redfern
is a rich open tweed."

Illustration 45. Costume designed and worn by Mrs. Jenness
Miller. "The suit consists of trousers, designed to look as much
like a divided skirt as possible, hanging from a sleeveless
underwaist, thus obviating the need of a belt at the waist. The
trousers are gathered to a band at the knee. The jacket is loose
and comfortable, with long, full skirt. Leggings of elastic cloth
reach to the knee. A cap of neat design completes the suit."

Illustration 47. Costume designed by Gosta Kraemer. "The costume consists of a medium plain skirt and a modification of the Eton jacket, with a soft roll collar and ends falling in front. With it is worn a dainty sweater or such waist as taste may dictate. The material may be serge, cravenette, or any of the soft woollens. Leggings of jersey cloth or other elastic material, with trousers under the skirt, are optional."

Illustration 46. Costume designed by Gosta Kraemer. "The trousers are of accordion-plaited serge, very full and gathered to a band buttoning at the knee, or an accordion-plaited skirt may be worn over knickerbockers, producing almost the same effect. The coat is single breasted, intended to button as shown or to hang almost closed when unbuttoned. A shirtwaist of wool or silk is worn under the coat. Leggings of jersey cloth, when desired, complete the costume."

Illustration 48. Costume designed by Redfern. "This is the costume for bicycling most favored in France. It consists of the famous bloomers, with Norfolk coat made of dark green tweeds, with collar and waist-band of green cloth of very deep shade fastened by gold buckles. The long gaiters are of slate colored cloth to match hat and gloves." *Kaufman Collection.*

Illustration 49. Bicycle costume designed and worn by Miss Georgia Cayvan. "This costume consists of Zouave trousers and a smart Eton jacket with full sleeves, worn over a skirt which may be either loose or close, or a dainty sweater or tight-fitting jersey bodice with or without sleeves. Around the waist is a belt of suede, drawn through a buckle. The trousers are made without lining and in light serges for summer, a warm lining being added for winter wear. Leggings of jersey cloth being elastic and affording full play to the ankles. A sailor hat, with chiffon at the side of Mercury wings, completes the costume." *McClelland Collection.*

Illustration 50. 4½in (11.5cm) tall,
each of the ladies from this set, *Lady
Cyclists Up to Date*, slips on and off
of her own bicycle. The lady on the
left is wearing a blue Eton jacket,
burgundy blouse and darker blue
trousers gathered in at the knee and
tan colored leggings. Her hat is dark
blue with a red feather. The lady on
the right is dressed in a similar Eton
jacket of bright pink with a green
blouse and dark blue trousers with
burgundy leggings. She is wearing a
pink, white and blue cap. All of the
pieces are deeply embossed and
richly colored. This set was printed
in Bavaria for the English trade.

Illustration 51. Lady Cyclists Up to Date — envelope.

LADIES OF THE SUNDAY ART SUPPLEMENT

In 1895, *The Boston Herald* and a number of other newspapers began a series of paper dolls to promote the sale of fashion patterns and increase their Sunday circulation. This series has often been referred to as the "Boston Herald Ladies" because it was first researched in that newspaper. The early costumes were numbered and dated but as the series continued, it appears that not every newspaper used all of the supplements, so after number 30, the numbers do not appear in all of the newspapers and many of the plates carry only a date. To make it even more confusing, different papers used different numbering and dating depending on when they began the series and which plates they chose to run. Unfortunately, once the costumes are cut out, all of this information is lost. It appears that all of the plates were lithographed by the G. H. Buck Company of New York and were sold to the various newspapers who then printed their own banners and other information on the sheets. To date the series is known to have appeared in *The Boston Sunday Herald*, *The Brooklyn Times*, the *Cincinnati Commercial Gazette*, *The Chicago Record*, *The New York Mercury*, *The Philadelphia Press*, the *Saint Louis Republic*, *The San Francisco Chronicle* and *The Washington Star*. The fashion figure in pink has also been found with advertising for imported Prima Donna Corsets printed on the back indicating that these ladies were also used as advertising premiums.

Illustration 52. Fashion figure in pink. The paper doll that began the series first appeared in *The Boston Sunday Herald* on March 24, 1895.

Illustration 53. Fashion figure in black. The second model appeared three months later, June 16, 1895.

Illustration 54. No. 1 "Ladies' Toilette," March 31, 1895. A black gown trimmed in pink combined with a black plumed hat decorated with pink flowers.

ABOVE RIGHT: Illustration 55. No. 2 "Ladies' Travelling Coat," April 7, 1895. A coat of rich brown covering a green dress, carrying a green and gold travel bag and including a matching brown hat with feathers.

RIGHT: Illustration 56. No. 3 "Ladies' Costume," April 14, 1895. A deep purple gown covered by a black cape decorated with lace and ribbons and a small hat in black trimmed with tiny purple flowers.

ABOVE LEFT: Illustration 57. No. 4 "Ladies Toilette," April 21, 1895. A dress of pink stripes on a white background with gray dots; the bodice is trimmed with white eyelet ruffles and pink ribbon. (No hat.)

ABOVE: Illustration 58. No. 4, "Ladies' Costume," November 1895, *The Philadelphia Press.* A brown and wine striped blouse combined with a brown jumper trimmed around the neckline and down the front in fur and carrying a matching fur muff. *Fertel Collection.*

Illustration 59. No. 5 "Ladies' Riding Habit," April 25, 1895. A black two-piece riding habit with a white blouse and black tie at the neck. (A black hat is not shown.)

LADIES' TOILETTE

PATTERNS OF THIS ELEGANT DESIGN CAN BE PROCURED FROM THE N.Y. MERCURY'S PATTERN DEPARTMENT
SEE COUPON IN THE SUNDAY MERCURY ACCOMPANYING THIS PLATE

THE CHICAGO RECORD.

MAY, 1895   WEEKLY COLORED COSTUME PLATE   No. 14

See The Chicago Record for descriptive and explanatory notes on this costume. A duplicate of this costume plate will be mailed to subscribers of the Chicago Record—and to none others—upon receipt of four cents, (two 2-cent stamps) to cover postage and mailing expenses. A duplicate of the "Model Figure" will also be sent upon the same terms

To fit Hat on Figure, cut on dotted Line

LADIES' OUTING SUIT.

Cut carefully around dress and tabs and secure to fashion figure by folding the tabs around back.

Illustration 61. No. 7, "Ladies Outing Suit," May 12, 1895. (No. 14, July 7, 1895, *The Chicago Record*.) "Blue and white striped linen duck makes this natty summer suit, the jacket revers being faced with plain blue linen. Belt and collar of white linen with blue silk four-in-hand necktie. White sailor hat, with blue ribbon band."* *Fertel Collection.*

Illustration 60. No. 6, "Ladies' Toilette," May 5, 1895. "An exquisite combination of Falstaff red satin with black silk is here shown, handsomely decorated with jet (beading). The black silk skirt is as full as fashion requires and plainly completed at the foot, the organ pipe in back being interlined with haircloth to give the stand out flare that is now in mode."*

A duplicate of the "Model Figure" will be mailed to subscribers of the Boston Sunday Herald upon receipt of four cents (two 2 cent stamps) to cover postage and mailing expenses.

Illustration 62. No. 8, "Ladies' Toilette," May 19, 1895. "A stylish combination of two tone vicuna with emerald green satin with revers on jacket of Bengaline, darker shade of gray, with steel blue buttons."*

Illustration 63. No. 8, "Ladies' Wrapper and Infant Robe," June 16, 1895, *Cincinnati Commercial Gazette.* "Scrimp [sic] pink cashmere made this dainty wrapper which is handsomely decorated with white lace, and bust girdle with bow and long ends of satin ribbons a darker shade of pink. The infant's robe can be made from nainsook, cambric, or lawn and can be trimmed with fine embroidery."*

LADIES TOILETTE

THE SUNDAY HERALD.
MAY, 26, 1895. WEEKLY COLORED COSTUME PLATE. No. 9.

LADIES' EVENING TOILETTE.

Illustration 65. No. 10, "Ladies' Toilette," June 2, 1895. "This stylish toilette depicts a striking combination of Sans Gene and cream colored striped crepel-de soie with velvet and chiffon of the same rich shade of mauve. The waist is decorated with a handsome yoke of jet passementarie and a blouse front of plaited chiffon. Rosettes are of mauve velvet. The sleeves are very full at the top, and fitting the arm below the elbow."*

Illustration 64. No. 9, "Ladies' Evening Toilette," May 26, 1895. "The mode portrays the fancy for separate waists and skirts, which will continue in vogue throughout the season. Pink silk crepe is chosen for this charming waist, the skirt being of black crepon in fancy weave."*

35

Illustration 66. No. 11, "Young Ladies Yachting Toilette," June 9, 1895. "This stylish design is extremely nautical and up-to-date. Navy blue vicuna is the material represented, the collar, belt, and trimming being of white faced cloth, decorated with gilt braid."*

ABOVE RIGHT: Illustration 67. No. 12, "Garden Party Toilette," June 23, 1895. "Ladies' waist with Star Collar and Pipe Organ Skirt - The charming toilette here illustrated is admirable for a lawn fete, country dance, afternoon visiting or carriage wear. Ivory white, brocaded silk is the handsome material chosen, the crush collar and belt being of corn-flower blue velvet. The fanciful yoke collar, cut in star points, is made of blue silk, covered with lace, forming epaulettes over the fashionable full-topped sleeves."*

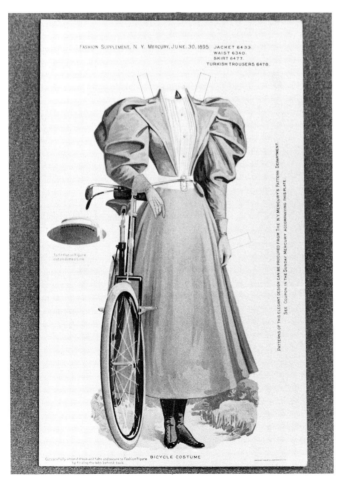

LEFT: Illustration 68. No. 13, "Bicycle Costume," June 30, 1895. "This suit, of tan colored cloth, consists of a belted Eton jacket, which is worn over a white shirt waist of Madres, and a full gored skirt of ample width, which is worn over Turkish trousers, and gaiters of the same material. The belt is of white canvas, with silver buckle, and a black satin stock bow is worn at the neck. Gray driving gloves and white straw sailor hat complete the costume."*

Illustration 69. No. 14 "Ladies' Bathing Suit," July 7, 1895. Navy blue swimsuit trimmed with a white collar, white braid and a red sash. (A red bathing cap is not shown.)

ABOVE RIGHT: Illustration 70. No. 15, July 14, 1895. A penoir made of pale yellow fabric with black dots and trimmed with wide lace over a pleated yellow nightie.

RIGHT: Illustration 71. No. 16, July 21, 1895. A three-piece traveling suit with a tan jacket and skirt combined with a tan and white pinstriped blouse and a black tie at the neck.

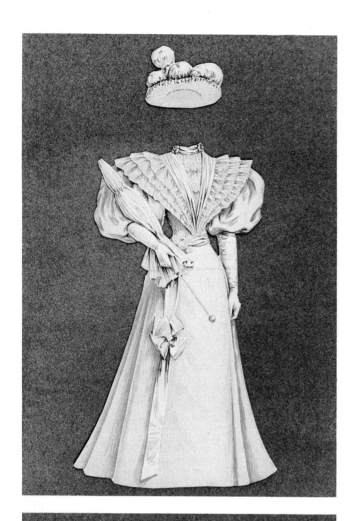

ABOVE LEFT: Illustration 72. No. 17 "Ladies' Seaside Toilette," July 28, 1895. A cream-colored gown with ruffling over the shoulders trimmed with white ribbon including a white parasol and a wide hat decorated with white plumes.

ABOVE: Illustration 73. No. 18 "Ladies' Casino Toilette," August 4, 1895. An elegant gown of pale green print fabric, the bodice and lower sleeves are white with yellow trim and small ruffles; includes a white parasol. (A pale green hat with black plumes is not shown.)

Illustration 74. No. 19 "Ladies' Afternoon Toilette," August 11, 1895. A pink gown trimmed with white shirred fabric at the neck and white lace flounces over the shoulder accented with dark pink ribbon bows and rosettes. (No hat.)

Illustration 75. No. 20 "Ladies' Demi Toilette," August 18, 1895. A gown of gray and white striped fabric with a cream colored bodice accented with purple and black beading and purple ribbon trimming at the waist and neckline. (No hat.)

ABOVE RIGHT: Illustration 76. No. 21, "Wedding Gown," August 25, 1895. A cream colored gown with a white shirred capelet collar with a floor-length veil trimmed with tiny white flowers. *Fertel Collection.*

RIGHT: Illustration 77. No. 22, "Bridesmaid's Toilette," September 1, 1895. A pale pink gown with beaded epaulettes over the shoulder; carrying a bouquet of pink roses attached to a wide white ribbon; the matching hat is pale gray with black plumes and a pink rose. *Fertel Collection.*

Illustration 78. No. 23, "Ladies Walking Toilette," September 8, 1895. A black suit accented with a red and green plaid blouse and matching revers on the jacket and a hat of black with red and green feathers.

Illustration 79. No. 24, "Ladies' Driving or Dust Coat," September 15, 1895. A chestnut brown double-breasted coat with a dark brown collar and a matching brown hat with two dark brown plumes.

Illustration 81. No. 26, "Ladies' Opera Toilette," September 29, 1895. A gown of lime green with white flounces decorating the neckline, sleeves and hemline; a purple nosegay accents the collar.

Illustration 80. No. 25, "Ladies' Toilette," September 22, 1895. A black cape trimmed with black fur and jet beads covering a cream colored gown patterned with gray and including a matching cream colored hat with plumes, ribbon bow and a buckle.

Illustration 82. No. 27, "Ladies' English Jacket Suit," October 6, 1895. The jacket and skirt are dark brown flecked with blue; the wide collar of the jacket is blue; beneath is a plain brown double-breasted waistcoat and a white blouse with a tiny blue collar; the matching hat is brown with blue bows.

Illustration 83. No. 28, "Ladies' Redingote Costume," October 13, 1895. "The stylish gown of redingote variety, is of dark green broadcloth, made over a front gore and chemisette of dark green brocade silk, showing a pink figure in its weave. The crush collar is of pink velvet to match the figure in shade, and the large reverse collar and deep slashed elbow cuffs are of dark green velvet. Handsome cut steel buttons furnish decoration AND close the double-breasted fronts of the pointed waist."*

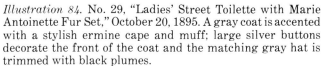

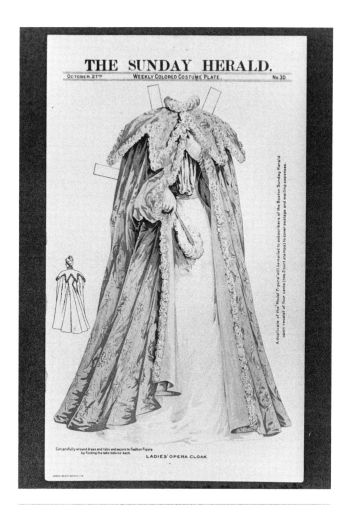

Illustration 84. No. 29, "Ladies' Street Toilette with Marie Antoinette Fur Set," October 20, 1895. A gray coat is accented with a stylish ermine cape and muff; large silver buttons decorate the front of the coat and the matching gray hat is trimmed with black plumes.

ABOVE RIGHT: Illustration 85. No. 30 "Ladies' Opera Cloak," October 27, 1895. A chartreuse brocade cloak trimmed in white with a star-pointed capelet and lined in pink covering a white gown.

RIGHT: Illustration 86. No. 39, "Ladies' Carriage Toilette," October 1895, *The Chicago Record*. A brown fur cloak covers a purple gown trimmed with black jet. (A purple hat is not shown.)

ABOVE LEFT: Illustration 87. No. 40, "Debutante Toilette," October 1895, *The Chicago Record.* An all white gown with white ruffles and rosettes at the neckline and a white sash at the waist; carrying pink roses.

ABOVE: Illustration 88. No. 41, "Ladies' Day Reception Toilette," November 1895, *The Chicago Record.* A white jacket with brocaded red roses covers a white and gold print blouse which is joined at the waist by a red sash to a plain black skirt. (A black hat with pink flowers is not shown.)

Illustration 89. No. 43 "Ladies' Calling Costume," November 1895. The blue and yellow patterned fabric of the skirt and bodice is combined with matching plain blue sleeves; black and blue braid trims the sleeves, waist and bodice; the bodice, itself, is pleated in bright yellow. (A blue hat is not shown.)

Illustration 90. No. 44, "Ladies' Matinee Toilette," November 1895. A gown of a dark green fabric patterned in a white figure accented with a brighter green collar trimmed in ermine fur and the ermine is repeated at the waistline and at the bottom of the sleeve.

ABOVE RIGHT: Illustration 91. January 5, 1896. A wine red suit in a diagonal weave is richly trimmed with brown fur over the shoulders, down the front, at the bottom of the sleeves, and at the hem; a fur muff and ice skates are included and the matching hat is of black plumes and a red and black bow.

RIGHT: Illustration 92. "Ladies' English Tailor Gown," January 12, 1896. A two-piece gown of a dull brown patterned fabric trimmed with military braid of gold and black, and a matching hat of brown with a black feather.

ABOVE LEFT: Illustration 93. "Ladies' Princess Toilette," January 19, 1896. A bright wine colored coat-dress with bodice and sleeves in a coordinated fabric patterned with black with green highlights and trimmed with black fur at the neck and carrying a matching muff. The hat is also wine with black plumes.

ABOVE: Illustration 94. "Ladies' Luncheon Toilette," January 26, 1896. Iridescent emerald green fabric in the gown is accented with white lace set in the bodice. The matching hat is green with a black bow.

Illustration 95. "Ladies' Afternoon Toilette," February 2, 1896. Rich, deep purple is combined with a bodice of orange and white brocade and deep orange and purple ribbon trims the waist and sleeves.

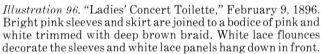

Illustration 96. "Ladies' Concert Toilette," February 9, 1896. Bright pink sleeves and skirt are joined to a bodice of pink and white trimmed with deep brown braid. White lace flounces decorate the sleeves and white lace panels hang down in front.

ABOVE RIGHT: Illustration 97. "Ladies' Home Toilette," February 16, 1896. A gold and white brocade waist with pink insert in front is combined with a black skirt and the bodice, waistline and sleeves are trimmed with red ribbons.

RIGHT: Illustration 98. "Ladies' Demi-Evening Toilette," February 23, 1896. A white brocade jacket trimmed with red roses over a white shirred blouse combined with a lime green skirt.

ABOVE LEFT: Illustration 99. Unidentified. A brown costume with the cape trimmed with black shirred fabric topped with a white star collar and a touch of fur at the neck including a brown parasol enhanced with white lace trim and dark blue bow. (A brown hat is not shown.)

ABOVE: Illustration 100. No. 6, "Ladies' Toilette," March, 1895, *The Chicago Record.* A three-piece costume, the jacket and skirt in blue trimmed with a wide pink collar and matching pink bows on the sleeves and at the hem, white lace under the collar on the lower sleeves and down the front. The blouse is white with pleats and tiny pink buttons for trim. (A white lace hat is not shown.)

Illustration 101. No. 7, "Ladies' Toilette," *The Chicago Record.* A blue and white striped dress shirred at the neck with lace trim over the shoulders and carrying an open parasol of dark blue edged in wide lace and a small black bag. (A gray hat with black plumes is not shown.)

Illustration 102. No. 5, "Ladies' Corsage," March, 1895, *The Chicago Record.* A brown gown accented with a front panel of chartreuse green and matching brown bows at the shoulders, neck and waist and holding sheet music. (No hat.)

ABOVE RIGHT: Illustration 103. Unidentified. A gown made of blue fabric dotted with black, trimmed with lace across the top of the bodice and accented with black ribbon down the front of the dress and at the neck.

RIGHT: Illustration 104. Unidentified. A two-piece costume of dark purple trimmed across the front and on the sleeves with violet inserts enhanced with braid and edged with black fur. The fur is also repeated at the hem; carrying a matching black fur muff.

Other costumes not pictured:

— An ecru gown with white lace panels down the skirt front, accented with a white lace collar over pink; a wide pink sash at the waist and carrying a feather fan.

— A gown of bright green fabric woven with red and pink iridescent flowers with a white lace jabot at the neck and a vest with a red and green design over a gray background and edged with black ruching.

— A pale yellow gown with yellow, green and red plaid fabric accenting the bodice and sleeves; shown walking a dog.

— A gray dress with buttons down the front and accents in pink.

— A rose penoir trimmed with wide lace over a pink night gown.

— A black beaded lace bodice covers a cream blouse and is combined with a deep blue skirt.

*These descriptions have been taken directly from various newspapers that carried the supplement sheets and the accompanying pattern information.

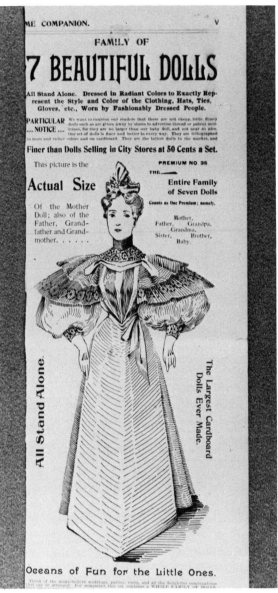

Illustration 105. Advertisement for the MC&K dolls shows that they were used as premiums for subscribing to *Ladies' Home Companion. McClelland Collection.*

BELOW: Illustration 106. The MC&K Family of paper dolls is from left to right marked: *Grandfather, Grandmother, Father, Mother, Sister, Brother* and *Baby Sister.* The dolls come in two pieces. The costumes are cut double and slip over the head, shoulders and arms. They are beautifully lithographed in full color and only marked, "Copyrighted, 1895, by M.,C.& K., 108 Times Building, New York."

THE HOOD'S FAMILY

The C. I. Hood's Company of Lowell, Massachusetts, offered an entire family of five paper dolls to promote their patent medicine. The set includes 19 pieces, all in beautiful full color. Each doll has two extra costumes and appropriate hats. The back of each doll and costume is covered with advertising claims. This set of dolls comes in several variations. In all of the sets the dolls are the same. In the first variation, which is fully pictured, the dolls and clothing were completely die-cut; only the hats were to be cut out. In the second variation each doll is still die-cut but special cutting instructions also appear on the front. "Cut through the card on heavy black outlines of whiskers" is on the chest of the father.

"Cut through ruffle on heavy black outlines" is printed on Mother's camisole. The hats for the daughters which accompany this set are different not only in design, but they were produced by a three-color process rather than the full four-color one. The clothing is exactly the same as the pictured set. Finally, the third variation is strikingly different. It appears that the company wanted to update the set by designing a new wardrobe with the latest turn-of-the-century fashions. Only one costume — Father's tan coat with the box of Hood's Sarsparilla sticking out of the pocket - remains as in the former sets. Still the dolls and the clothing are die-cut and the hats remain for the child to cut out.

Illustration 107. *Father* and *Mother* from the *Hood's Family* with their extra costumes. (First variation.)

Illustration 108. The two sisters above and the brother below, from the *Hood's Family* with their extra costumes. (First variation.)

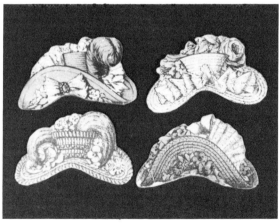

Illustration 109. The little girl's hats from the second variation. *Edgar Collection.*

Illustration 110. The family from the third variation. Notice cutting instructions on the front of each doll which also appears on the second variation. *McClelland Collection.*

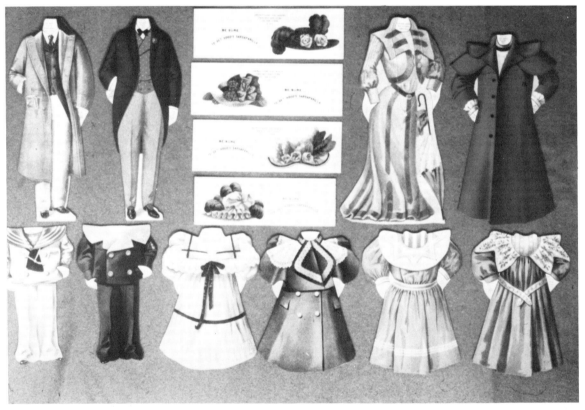

ABOVE: Illustration 111. The clothing from the third variation. *McClelland Collection.*

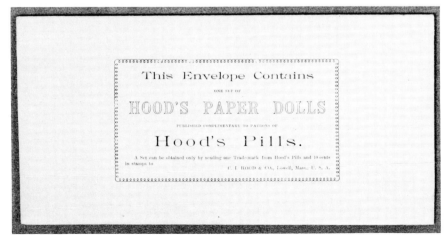

Illustration 112. Hood's envelope. *McClelland Collection.*

Victorian Children

Toys, games, children's books — the very concept of childhood, itself began to emerge only a few hundred years ago during the Middle Ages. Before this time children were viewed as miniature adults. Once past infancy, they joined with their elders. Children and adults wore the same clothes, worked at the same tasks and played the same games. They were immediately exposed to all aspects of adult life. The word "child" itself indicated relationship, not one's age. Parents did not record a child's age, and because infant mortality was so high, society did not value children as individually important.

With the Victorians, especially in the middle and upper classes, important attitude changes toward children were developing. The Victorians held high religious ideals. Christianity taught that children were born innocent and vulnerable, but inherently sinful. Parents had an obligation from birth to raise their children, educating them and disciplining them to save them from sin. Life was a constant battle with the devil, and only by learning self-restraint could children be protected from temptation.

In the more affluent households children were separated completely from adults. They were placed in nurseries to be raised by their nannies, spending time with their parents only when summoned. Children were disciplined severely and fed austere foods. Other young boys and girls did not live at home but were sent away to boarding schools where they were strictly regulated. Young girls were carefully protected to preserve their innocence. The great emphasis on educating children against inherited sin led to the organization of an entire network of educational institutions and mass education of the middle and upper classes.

The early Victorian paper dolls were designed to be instructional. Sometimes they included short stories teaching a moral, and often they provided comments instructing the child in proper dress. Many of these early paper dolls came in booklet form. Proper young ladies were encouraged to take up parlor crafts — needlework, drawing, painting. Some young women created handmade paper dolls; others carefully cut out and put together the commercially printed ones.

In America, John McLoughlin founded a printing business in 1828. He was a wood engraver and he was interested in good printing. He immediately began to publish children's books. By mid century his two sons, John Jr. and Edmund, had taken over the business forming McLoughlin Brothers. They produced all kinds of printed materials for children. They are one of the earliest and probably most successful American publishing company to print paper dolls. But the company has been best known for its children's books. The company printed eight-page books that sold for a penny, and ten-page books in two colors for two cents. They also made doll houses and furniture, lithographed blocks — nesting, picture blocks and building blocks. They wanted to keep up large sales at low cost so the books and games that they produced were "old favorites" and out of copyright so there were no royalties to pay. Their paper dolls ranged in price from inexpensive, penny folders to 20 cents for something special like *Ida Mae* or *Little Red Riding Hood*.

Other American firms also produced paper dolls like Peter Thomson Company of Cincinnati, Ohio; Brown, Taggard and Chase of Boston, Massachusetts; and Clark, Austin, & Smith of New York, but none could match the quantity produced by the McLoughlin Brothers.

In 1867, E. G. Selchow and John H. Righter joined as partners in a publishing business. The company has been best known for the timeless games that it has produced. *Parcheesi* and *Scrabble* have been popular for over 100 years. Much less is known about their paper dolls. Selchow and Righter acted as manufacturers' agents to market many toys and games. Because the style of their paper dolls is so varied, and because, from time to time, we see some of the same paper dolls marked by other publishers, it is probable that they also acted as agents and marketed paper dolls for other smaller companies. Regretably, the envelopes from their paper dolls give us little information about them and about how many sets of paper dolls they published. The paper dolls are really charming and certainly must have aimed to compete with R. Tuck.

By the mid 1870s, a period of tremendous growth was beginning that would extend into the 20th century. With it came an ever increasing material wealth. During this time some very lavish paper dolls were made. In Germany, wonderful, full color, embossed paper dolls were being turned out in sheets to be cut and in deluxe boxed sets that were die-cut.

In England, publishing companies like Dean and Son Limited, J. W. Spear (noted for their parlor games), and, of course, R. Tuck and Sons began producing elaborate paper dolls early in the 1890s. It is interesting to note that in the earliest sets often the design work was done in England, but printing was frequently done in Bavaria.

With growing middle class affluence and increasing literacy, companies discovered the value of advertising. The 1890s became the "Golden Age" of advertising. Society was deluged with trade cards and all kinds of paper advertising gimmicks including the advertising paper doll. Soap, dye, coffee, thread, patent medicine and just about everything else offered paper dolls and other paper toys to entice people to try their products.

The paper dolls also recorded the fashions for children which were no longer mere copies of their parents' clothing. It was proper to dress children according to their age. Babies and toddlers wore full, flowing infant gowns. A girl's skirt length was determined by her age; the length of a boy's trousers, by his age. Until the age of six little boys were dressed in skirts and looked just like the little girls. Little girls from the age of three to five wore dresses with empire waists.

As little boys grew older, they began to wear trousers called "knickerbockers" — they were baggy pants which ended in a band at the knee. For dress they added a jacket creating "knickerbocker suits, sailor suits, or blazer suits, which were often for school." Velvet dress suits with shirts trimmed with wide white lace collars became the "Little Lord Fauntleroy" look in the eighties. Knee pants became fashionable in the nineties.

In the sixties, fashions for little girls were very much like their mothers; dresses had wide necklines, narrow waists and large sleeves. Girls wore straw bonnets whenever they went out. Tailored suits also came into fashion. In the 1870s, the bustle was introduced. At first on the little girl's dresses it began as a large bow; later, it became an overskirt which was pulled up and puffed out.

During the eighties it was fashionable to starch dresses, pinafores, aprons, shirts and other garments to give that clean, fresh look. Starch was not expensive so any mother could give her child that fresh,

Illustration 113. 6⅜in (16.1cm) *Myra Mild* was produced by the McLoughlin Brothers. She is part of a series of nine paper dolls printed in three sizes which was sold in the 1870s. These paper dolls have lovely soft colors. The clothes are printed front and back. *Myra Mild* is one of the middle size dolls. She originally sold for ten cents.

crisp look. At this time children's clothing was inspired by naval uniforms as the American government began to expand its naval forces. Both boys and girls wore sailor suits. This motif extended into the next century as the Spanish-American War of 1898 reinforced the interest in the navy.

Another interesting development — the beginning of the mail order business in the 1870s — had a great effect on children's clothing. By the 1890s, catalogs offered fashions that were not more than a season old.

By the end of the period children, like the adults, were beginning to wear more comfortable and practical clothing. Knitting machines were developed and the sweater was introduced. Brownie suits gave the idea for the bib-overalls to children.

Illustration 115. 4⅝in (11.8cm) *Mollie* was published by McLoughlin Brothers but does not appear listed on the back of her folder. She is very much like other paper dolls in "Series No. 2. 12 kinds." It is believed that she came in booklet form with four outfits to cut out, but the number of hats is uncertain.

Illustration 114. Myra Mild — envelope.

LEFT: Illustration 116. Susie's Pets — folder. McClelland Collection.

Illustration 117. 6⅜in (16.1cm) *Susie's Pets* was first published by McLoughlin Brothers in 1858. Originally, the set came in sheets to cut out. *Susie's* wardrobe includes five outfits and one hat printed front and back. This is one of the few early McLoughlin sets to include front and back clothing. (The hat is not pictured.)

ABOVE: *Illustration 118.* 4in (10.2cm) *Sallie* was published by the Thomson Company of Cincinnati, Ohio, probably in the 1880s. Uncut, she came folded, and when opened out, she had three costumes and hats, front only, to cut out.

LEFT: *Illustration 119.* 4¾in (12.2cm) each, these three children, now cut out, were embossed and printed in Germany in sheets. Done in deep, rich colors, they depict children gardening.

Illustration 120. This uncut sheet printed in Germany shows a lavish birthday party. Notice that the extra clothing does not have tabs. The sheet probably dates from the 1870s.

Illustration 121. An uncut sheet of dancers, also probably produced in Germany. This sheet is unusual because its deep, rich colors are accented with gold.

Illustration 122. Another similar uncut sheet of dancers, probably from Germany, is a little different because it is marked as two pages and the dolls and clothing are all front and back.

Illustration 123. This uncut advertising card was produced by the Domestic Sewing Machine Company. *McClelland Collection.*

Illustration 124. 13in (33cm) *Dear Dorothy,* Artistic Series 500, has brown hair and blue eyes. She wears a white camisole and a purple petticoat. She is shown with hat A (center) white with pink flowers and pink ribbons, costume C (left) red coat with ermine fur trim and a matching red hat with dark blue feathers, and costume D (right) green coat with brown trim and ivory lace.

DOLLS FOR ALL SEASONS

These beautiful paper dolls each came with four costumes — one for each season of the year. They were produced by the R. Tuck company in two sizes. The large size dolls came in boxes. These dolls have the Tuck patented heads. The smaller size came in a paper envelope and these dolls have slits in their shoulders to accommodate dress tabs. All four dolls appear in both sizes and in both series the dolls and dresses are die-cut. The series was designed by Margaret McDonald who created many of the early Tuck paper dolls. Each doll is marked "By Special Appointment Publishers to Her Majesty the Queen, Raphael Tuck and Sons London, Paris, New York, Designed at the studios in New York and printed at the Fine Arts Works in Bavaria."

Illustration 125. 13in (33cm) *Rosey Ruth,* Artistic Series 501, has light hair and blue eyes. She is wearing a white camisole and a blue petticoat. She is shown with costume A (upper left) a dark red dress trimmed in midnight blue with yellow dots and other accents of yellow and a matching dark red hat trimmed with blue feathers and flowers, costume B (upper right) a pink and white dress trimmed with pink ribbons and ruffles and a natural straw hat trimmed with red and pink roses, costume C (lower left) a green coat decorated with ermine fur including a muff and matching green hat with white plumes and a purple bow, costume D (lower right) a dress of light blue with a delicate white design trimmed with white ruffles and a large dark blue bow and matching hat of natural straw trimmed with white feathers and blue bows.

Illustration 126. 13in (33cm) *Merry Marion*, Artistic Series 502, has light hair and brown eyes. She wears a white camisole and a yellow petticoat. She is shown with costume A (upper left) a dark red ensemble with a red and white striped skirt topped with a brown jacket and carrying a doll. The matching hat is red with red and white plumes and a striped bow. Costume B (upper right) a white dress covered by a dark blue coat trimmed in brown fur and a matching blue hat with white feathers and a gold bow, costume C (lower left) a purple dress trimmed in yellow and deep purple ribbons. The matching hat is natural straw with purple ribbons and plumes. Costume D (lower right) is green with white dots, trimmed with white ruffles with red dots and yellow stripes bound in red and white lace. Her hat is of natural straw with a red ribbon, green feathers and daisies.

Illustration 127. Sweet Alice, Artistic Series 503, has brown hair and eyes. She is wearing a white camisole trimmed in pink and a pink petticoat. She is shown with costume A (upper left) a yellow blouse with purple dots and a purple skirt trimmed in yellow and green. Her matching hat is green with purple and yellow ribbons. Costume B (upper right) is yellow with white ruffles and a blue ribbon. The matching hat is yellow with a white ruffle and a blue bow. Costume C (lower left) is a red cape trimmed in black fur over a gray striped ensemble with a red hat with black feathers and fur. Costume D (lower right) is light blue with a white pinafore. The matching hat is white with blue bows. *McClelland Collection.*

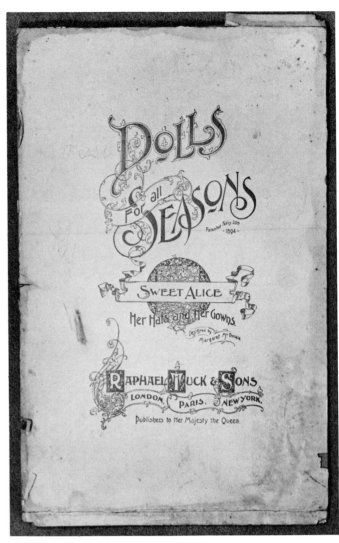

*Illustration 128. Sweet Alice — box lid.
McClelland Collection.*

LEFT: Illustration 129. Two sizes compared. The doll on the left measures 13in (33cm), the one on the right 9in (22.9cm).

SELCHOW AND RIGHTER

This company was formed in 1863 and gained its early reputation for its parlor games which were so popular with the Victorians. Two of their most famous games — *Scrabble* and *Parchesi* — are still popular today. The company not only published its own products but also acted as a manufacturers' agent, marketing toys and games and paper dolls for other smaller companies. This explains why other publishers' names also appear on the same paper dolls and why there is such diversity in the style of the Selchow and Righter paper dolls.

Selchow and Righter marketed a series of paper dolls in tan paper envelopes that are only marked,

"Published by SELCHOW & RIGHTER, New York." There are several series in different sizes. The dolls that show up most frequently are 9in (22.9cm). The dolls are unmarked but the tabs on the dresses are numbered. The numbers are in two parts. For instance, *Mamie's* dress is 4-1. This means that the doll's number is 4. Each of *Mamie's* dresses bears the number 4. It is also costume number 1. Each of the dolls has three costumes with three matching hats. What makes this difficult is that the company is not consistent. Sometimes the doll number appears first and sometimes the costume number is first. The hats are also unmarked.

Illustration 130. 9in (22.9cm) *Mamie* has brown hair and brown eyes. She is dressed in a white petticoat trimmed with pink ribbon. Her costumes are from left to right: 1-4 a yellow and red plaid dress with a red and white striped insert in the bodice and a yellow hat trimmed with pink ribbon; 2-4 a dark red dress with a wide white collar and a green bow at the neck with matching green cuffs and a green band above the hem and a hat of green with yellow ribbon and gray plumes; 4-3 a steel blue dress trimmed with gold buttons and gold braid with a matching blue hat with gold ribbon and white plumes.

Illustration 131. 9in (22.9cm) *Flossie* has brown hair and brown eyes and is holding a pink rose. She is dressed in a white petticoat trimmed with blue ribbon. Her costumes are from left to right: 1-5 a red ruffled dress with a yellow ribbon at the waist; 5-2 a blue dress, trimmed with dark pink ribbon, with a white insert at the neck and white lower sleeves; 5-3 a green dress with a white collar and insert trimmed in dark blue, and matching dark blue decoration on the skirt. (The three hats are not pictured.)

Illustration 132. 9in (22.9cm) *Katie* has light hair and blue eyes and she has a blue bow in her hair. She is dressed in a white petticoat trimmed with pink ribbon. Her costumes are from left to right: 6-1 a deep blue dress with a light blue collar and a red ribbon sash, and a yellow hat decorated with red and pink ribbons; 6-2 a red dress with a wide band of blue and yellow trim down the front and a black belt and a matching yellow hat tgrimmed with red ribbon and black plumes; 6-3 a pink dress with a wide lace collar and a yellow hat trimmed with yellow and pink roses, a pink bow and a matching pink plume.

OUR FAVORITE DOLLS

These wonderful, big paper dolls bring up many questions. Who printed these dolls? Were they printed by more than one company? Were they pirated? Or were they just marketed by different agents who were permitted to put their own name on them? Basically, there are a boy and a girl, each with several printing variations. The two girl dolls when compared, although they have different faces, are both cut from the same die. They are even printed identically from the neck down. Similarly, the two boy dolls have different faces but are also die-cut identically from the neck down. However, because of changes to the hair, the die-cuts of the two boy dolls do not line up above the neck. Each doll has five outfits and five matching hats except for the one girl produced by the Amlico Company, which has only four outfits and four hats.

These dolls all come in folders which are printed in two different color combinations — green and purple on white, and yellow and purple on white. (The purple is sometimes faded and appears brown.) Some of the folders are marked and some are unmarked. The only dolls and clothes that are marked read, "A.T.Co." (It is possible that "A.T.Co." stands for American Three-Color Company which incorporated with several other small companies to become the American Colortype Company.) They come in unmarked folders. Selchow and Righter marketed these dolls in the yellow, purple and white folders with their name on the front. However, these folders also appear unmarked. Were these marketed by Selchow and Righter? To date, both variations of the boy and girl have been found in the yellow, purple and white folders.

The set marked "Amlico" (which probably stands for American Lithograph Company) has been found in both the green, purple and white folder and the yellow, purple and white folder. The doll and her clothes are of the same design but the clothes appear in different colors than in the other sets.

Illustration 133. The doll's envelope, which is printed in yellow and purple on white, is marked "Published by Selchow & Righter 267 Canal St, N.Y." and below "American Litho Co. N.Y."

Illustration 134.
16½in (41.9cm) girl with light brown hair, center-parted, is wearing a white petticoat. On the left is a dress with a red and yellow plaid bodice, a burgundy colored vest trimmed with fur and a skirt of pale blue with pink and blue bows, and a matching plaid tam. On the right is a pink dress with blue dots trimmed with blue ribbons covered by a white pinafore which is drawn up to hold a mixed bouquet of wild flowers. The matching hat is pink with red, blue and white flowers.

BELOW: Illustration 135. The dress on the left is a dark blue sailor dress with gold anchors on the lapels and a gold belt. The blouse is red and white striped with a white collar. The matching hat is dark blue with a white band. The dress in the middle is light blue with a white insert in front and white lace around the collar and cuffs. The dress and matching hat of natural straw are trimmed with orange and purple ribbons. The dress on the right is rose colored trimmed with white lace and chartreuse ribbon rosettes. (A matching rose colored hat is not shown.)

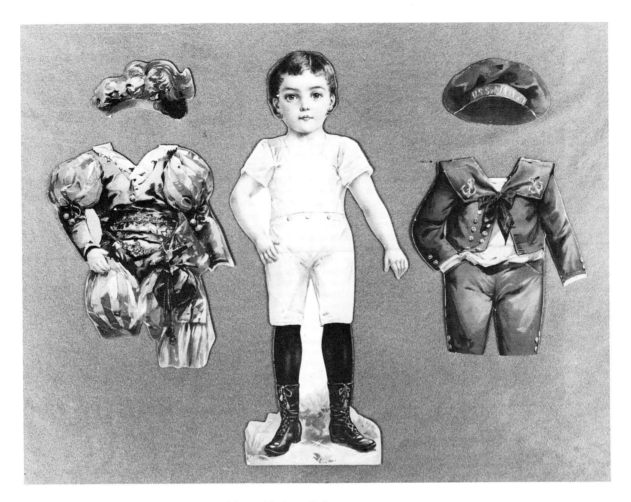

ABOVE: *Illustration 136.* 17in (43.2cm) boy with short, light brown hair is wearing white underwear. On the left is a turquoise outfit with red and yellow striped sleeves and legs trimmed with gold and wearing a gold sword, and a matching hat in red and blue with red plumes. On the right is a rose-colored sailor suit trimmed with gold buttons and anchors worn with a pale yellow and blue striped shirt and a matching cap.

BELOW: *Illustration 137.* The outfit on the left is a Scottish highland costume with a burgundy jacket and a red plaid skirt and a red and blue plaid scarf over the shoulder. The outfit in the center is a navy blue military suit and the outfit on the right is taken from a French Zouave uniform. The jacket is red trimmed with gold braid and the pants are blue with a yellow sash. (Hats for these outfits are not shown.)

Illustration 138. 16½in (41.9cm) girl with light brown hair is wearing a white petticoat. The dress in the upper left is blue with yellow ribbons and rosettes and a straw hat trimmed with pink roses and a blue feather; the dress in the upper right is pink with a green sash and green ribbon trim and a matching hat of yellow with blue and green ribbons. In the lower left is a yellowish-green dress covered by a white pinafore, drawn up, holding flowers and a hat with mixed flowers, and the dress in the lower left is pink with a plaid bodice and sleeves combined with a matching plaid tam. *Fertel Collection.*

Illustration 139. The doll's envelope is printed in green and purple on white and is marked, "Amlico publishing Company, 49 Barclay St, New York, U.S.A." (Amlico probably stands for American Litho Company.) *Fertel Collection.*

Illustration 140. The doll's envelope, which is printed in yellow and purple on white, is unmarked.

67

AMERICAN BEAUTIES

Very little is known about this series of paper dolls. The dolls come in buff envelopes. The printing is in dark green ink and reads "American Beauties" and their number.

Illustration 141. 9in (22.9cm) this little girl is *American Beauties No. 1.* She has blonde hair and blue eyes. She is wearing a white petticoat and red shoes and stockings. The dress in the upper left is light green trimmed with dark green and has a white blouse beneath and the matching hat is dark green accented with light green ribbon and a pink rose. The dress in the lower left is blue with pink stripes and a pink collar and cuffs and the hat is pink with pink ribbon. The dress on the right has a red jacket and bodice trimmed with black braid and a white skirt and the matching hat is black with red plumes and ribbon.

Illustration 142. American Beauties No. 1 — envelope.

Illustration 143. American Beauties No. 2 — envelope. Edgar Collection.

Illustration 144. 9in (22.9cm) this little girl is *American Beauties No. 2.* She has brown hair and dark eyes. She is wearing a red dress with black dots over a white blouse and black shoes and stockings. The dress on the left is pink with dark green collar and cuffs edged with fur. She is holding a doll. The matching hat is dark green with a pink plume. The dress on the upper right is red with a white pinafore and white lace collar and cuffs; the hat is all red. The dress on the lower left is lavender trimmed with deep purple ribbon and the matching hat is natural straw trimmed with purple. *Edgar Collection.*

DR. MILES' ADVERTISING DOLLS

The Dr. Miles' Medical Company of Elkart, Indiana, produced a full line of home remedies — Nervine, New Cure for the Heart, Restorative Tonic, and Blood Purifier — and advertised them with paper dolls which were over 21in (53.3cm) tall. Each doll was holding a giant bottle of one of its famous cure-alls. The dolls, as display, presumably sat on the druggist's counter. Instructions on the back of each paper doll stated that by sending one wrapper from any Dr. Miles' Remedy and five two-cent stamps, the doll and her costumes would be sent postpaid.

In 1899, the company offered *Grace* and *Edith*, each with three costumes and three hats. The dolls were published in beautiful, soft colors by the J. Ottmann Company of New York.

Illustration 145. 21⅜in (54.2cm) *Grace* has light hair and brown eyes. She wears a blue dress with a white collar and holds "Dr. Miles' Nervine." Costume No. 1 is a cloak with a muff and matching white fur-trimmed hood with wide blue ribbon, "To be worn on cold days."

Illustration 146. Costume No. 2 (on the left) "This is Grace's best dress and may be worn Sundays and to parties." The dress is red with a dark blue collar and cuffs, and has a yellow insert at the neck and a doll in its arms. The matching hat is white with black ribbon and plumes. Costume No. 3 (on the right) "School Dress" is white dotted material trimmed with white lace and holding a black Chinese fan with red trim. The hat is natural straw with a matching white bow.

Illustration 147. 21⅜in (54.2cm) *Edith* has black hair and dark blue eyes. She wears a blue sailor dress trimmed with a white collar, cuffs and braid. She holds a bottle of "Dr. Miles' Heart Cure." A straw sailor hat with a blue bow completes her outfit. Costume No. 1 (on the right) "Best Dress, To be worn to Church, School and Parties only." The dress is white with a wide red sash at the waist and blue ribbons on the skirt and around the sleeves. She holds a yellow rose. The matching bonnet is white with white plumes and a blue bow on top.

Illustration 148. Costume No. 2 (on the left) "House Dress. No hat with this dress." The dress is white with green stripes covered by a white apron. There is a red bow at the neck and she carries a large bowl of fruit. Costume No. 3 (on the right) "Rain Coat" is brown plaid with a dark blue umbrella. The matching plaid hat is not shown.

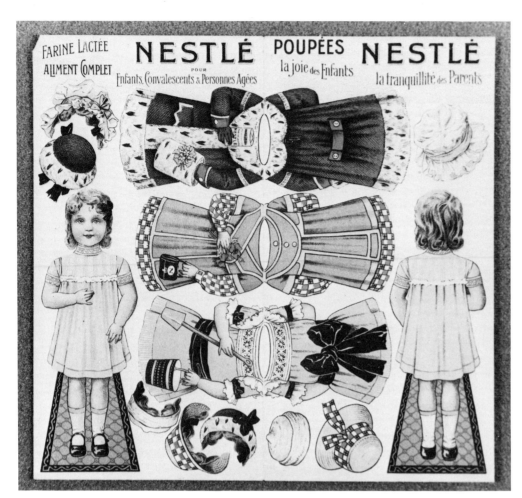

Illustration 149. An uncut advertising sheet with a paper doll produced by the Nestle Company and printed in French to promote their product in France. It probably dates from the 1890s. *McClelland Collection.*

Illustration 150. Another similar, uncut Nestle advertising sheet printed in French and used to promote their product in France during the 1890s. *McClelland Collection.*

Illustration 151. Grandmother's Tea Party was produced by the A&P Tea Company to promote its sales. The set consists of ten dolls and a tea table. "Grandmother" (in the front row, second from the left) was a symbol of the A&P Company for many years. *McClelland Collection.*

Illustration 152. The advertising flyer for *Grandmother's Tea Party* states that the full set is given away with a purchase of 50 cents. *McClelland Collection.*

Elegant Edwardians

Chapter 4

King Edward VII began his reign in 1901 amid a world of rapid social change. Factories were quickly becoming mechanized; labor unions were asserting themselves to improve working conditions and reduce working hours. Mass transit provided people with new mobility. With more opportunity for education, people were becoming more literate. Women were continuing their vigorous efforts to gain the right to vote and to have more freedom in public.

It is uncertain how much effect King Edward and his Queen, Alexandra, had on fashion but styles from this period have been labeled "Edwardian." After Victoria's long absence from the social scene, King Edward and beautiful Alexandra reigned for only ten years but they went everywhere, attending all of the great events of the English social calendar. People of wealth overlooked the social ills of the day and embraced a fanciful, romantic era of dress.

In an age when women were struggling to gain their rights, the new feminine fashions reflected the fact that women were still seen as just ornamental in a world dominated by men.

Illustrators like Charles Dana Gibson and Harrison Cady Fisher glorified the new silhouette that came to be referred to as the "Gibson Girl." This new look featured a long, sloping bust with a straight front and no hint of bosom or breast separation. The abdomen was pulled in, accentuating the small waist and completing the serpentine curve. This was all achieved by the use of a straight-fronted, constricting corset. The use of separates became popular. Dresses were often in two pieces; the blouses featured high necks and long, puffed sleeves. The long skirts were straight, but slightly flared. Small, close-fitting jackets completed the costume.

One of the classic examples of this famous "Gibson Girl" look appeared in the Sunday news supplements of the *Buffalo Sunday News* and *The Sunday Sun* (New York). It probably also appeared in other newspapers as well. The series has one doll and 13 costumes identified to date and was printed circa 1905. It is very realistic and in addition to entertaining the children, also served to promote patterns for the costumes which the newspapers offered for sale.

As the first decade of the 20th century progressed, the skirts no longer swept the floor and the fullness of the sleeves was modified. *Fanny Fairleigh*, produced by the R. Tuck Company, also shows the modifying trend of the latter part of the first decade. Hats, on the other hand, increased in size and trimming throughout the period. Flowers and feathers from exotic birds were especially fashionable. Hats grew so large in size that it was necessary to use large, decorative hat pins to secure them. Fur muffs and stoles also became important accessories, especially when accented with the animals' heads and tails. The lavish, extravagant use of furs and feathers led to important, early conservation laws by 1913.

Fluffy Ruffles was an entertaining example of the "Gibson Girl." She first appeared in the Sunday comic pages of *The New York Herald* in 1907, and instantly became the symbol of what the young American woman should be. The comic strip was a huge success, and was soon published in newspapers across the country. Drawn by Wallace Morgan, Fluffy Ruffles was an extremely beautiful woman who dressed with a most appealing flare. She distracted men so much that they could not work with her in the office. The comic strip showed her light-hearted attempts to hold one position after another, all failing because of her devastating effect on men. Her clothes were so stylish that they became accepted as the weekly symbol of what a young woman should wear. Retail stores nationwide began to feature "Fluffy Ruffles" sales and promote special "Fluffy Ruffles" outfits. In 1908, a "hit" song was published about her and soon a series of books was available. The comic strip ran for 14 months and finally ended on January 3, 1909. The *Fluffy Ruffles* paper doll, published by the Ottmann Litho Company, shows her stylish "Gibson Girl" influence.

As the Edwardian era progressed, women's clothing became less constricting. By 1910, the "no figure" silhouette was the look women wanted. Art Nouveau was having an impact on fashions and the trend was toward simplicity. Traces of oriental influence in line and strong color — red, green, yellow and orange — appeared. By 1914, hemlines had risen to eight inches from the floor. Women had more active lives and were beginning to reduce the number of layers of underclothing they wore. War on the European continent caused more serious attitudes and ended the frivolous, extravagant styles. Clothing became, by necessity, more practical as the war years progressed.

The *Mary Ware Doll Book* with its ten dolls and 38 costumes was first printed in 1914 and reflects well the fashions of the early teens. The book is hard bound with perforated pages. The paper dolls represent the characters and costumes from the books of the very popular "Little Colonel Series" for young women written by Annie Fellows Johnston. (The "Little Colonel" movie starring Shirley Temple was also taken from this series.) It is an unusual volume because the book is devoted totally to paper dolls and does not contain any written text. This volume is a companion to *The Little Colonel Doll Book* published in 1910.

After 1900, American magazines began to use more color in their printing, and as an added attraction to their readers often offered a full color paper doll page. *The Ladies Home Journal, The Delineator, Butterick* and others printed them regularly. Many of these paper dolls came with wardrobes of the latest fashions. With the increasing interest in sports, more appropriate clothes were being designed to accommodate the ladies' activities. In May and June of 1913 *The Delineator* magazine printed two pages which contrast the changes in fashion from 1903 to 1913.

By the close of this period the world was a very different place in which to live and the romance of the Edwardians was giving way to ever increasing pressure for modern social reform.

GIBSON GIRL OF THE SUNDAY NEWS

This paper doll and her wardrobe of 13 known costumes appeared in the *Buffalo Sunday News* and *The Sunday Sun* (New York) in 1905. Like the other fashion supplements, these pages were used to sell patterns and to boost newspaper sales by providing the ladies with the latest information about fashion trends. Readers were encouraged to use the other advertisements in the newspaper to help them find the material and trimmings for the garments. The pages were all produced by the American Litho Company of New York. The space at the top was left blank and each newspaper added its own banner. (The doll and her wardrobe from *McClelland Collection*.)

Illustration 153. The Fashion Model.

Illustration 154. Gown "with the New Vest Effect," February 12, 1905. Green plaid dress trimmed with black, featuring a gold vest and matching cuffs.

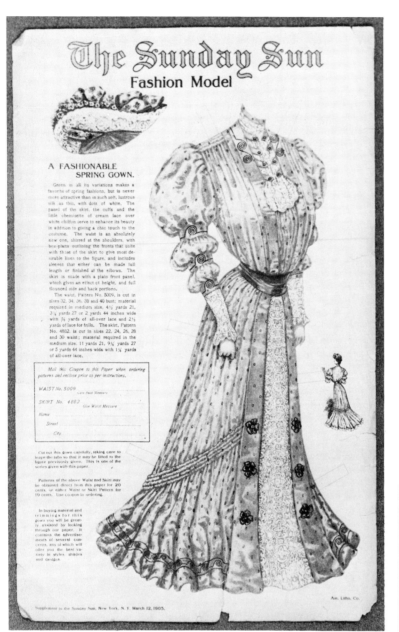

The Sunday Sun
Fashion Model

A FASHIONABLE SPRING GOWN.

Green in all its variations makes a favorite of spring fashions, but is never more attractive than in such soft, lustrous silk as this, with dots of white. The panel of the skirt, the cuffs and the little chemisette of cream lace over white chiffon serve to enhance its beauty in addition to giving a chic touch to the costume. The waist is an absolutely new one, shirred at the shoulders, with box-plaits outlining the fronts that unite with those of the skirt to give most desirable lines to the figure, and includes sleeves that either can be made full length or finished at the elbows. The skirt is made with a plain front panel, which gives an effect of height, and full flounced side and back portions.

The waist, Pattern No. 5009, is cut in sizes 32, 34, 36, 38 and 40 bust; material required in medium size, 4½ yards 21, 3¼ yards 27 or 2 yards 44 inches wide with ⅞ yards of all-over lace and 2½ yards of lace for frills. The skirt, Pattern No. 4882, is cut in sizes 22, 24, 26, 28 and 30 waist; material required in the medium size, 11 yards 21, 9¼ yards 27 or 5 yards 44 inches wide with 1½ yards of all-over lace.

Mail this Coupon to this Paper when ordering patterns and enclose price as per instructions.

WAIST No. 5009 .... *Give Bust Measure*

SKIRT No. 4882 .... *Give Waist Measure*

Name ....

Street ....

City ....

Cut out this gown carefully, taking care to leave the tabs so that it may be fitted to the figure previously given. This is one of the series given with this paper.

Patterns of the above Waist and Skirt may be obtained direct from this paper for 20 cents, or either Waist or Skirt Pattern for 10 cents. Use coupon in ordering.

In buying material and trimmings for this gown you will be greatly assisted by looking through our paper. It contains the advertisements of several concerns, any of which will offer you the best variety in styles, shades and designs.

Supplement to the Sunday Sun, New York, N. Y. March 12, 1905.

Am. Litho. Co.

Illustration 155. "A Fashionable Spring Gown," March 12, 1905. A soft green with white dots. The front panel and cuffs are cream colored lace over white.

Illustration 156. White gown with pink rosebuds, trimmed with a star point collar of lace and a green belt. Green braid and wide lace finish the hemline.

76

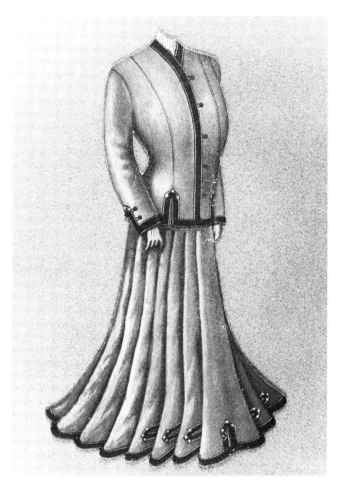

Illustration 157. The dark blue two-piece suit is trimmed in black braid.

ABOVE RIGHT: Illustration 158. A light blue gown with an ivory collar is accented with a white lace insert down the front and matching lace on the lower sleeve.

RIGHT: Illustration 159. A light green gown is trimmed with white lace cape collar and lace cuffs and accented with a darker green belt.

ABOVE LEFT: Illustration 160. Two-piece brown suit trimmed with dark brown braid is coordinated with a green and rust plaid vest.

ABOVE RIGHT: Illustration 161. A black three-quarter length coat covers a white blouse and a black and white checked skirt which is trimmed with black braid.

Illustration 162. A black gown is trimmed with ivory lace at the neck and in two bands on the skirt.

Illustration 163. A light blue gown is accented with midnight blue dots and a dark blue belt. The bodice and lower sleeve is trimmed with white lace.

ABOVE RIGHT: Illustration 164. Gray braid and a dark gray belt accent a gown of pale gray stripes and pink flowers on a white background.

RIGHT: Illustration 165. Red flowers on a white pleated gown are accented with red ribbon trim.

Not shown: Gown "for Morning Wear." A patterned robe with a little girl standing beside, also in her robe.

Illustration 166. Fluffy Ruffles — envelope.

Illustration 167. 10½in (26.7cm) *Fluffy Ruffles* published by the Ottmann Lithograph Company was based on a character that was designed by Wallace Morgan for *The New York Herald* (copyright 1907) and appeared in the comics. The doll has blonde hair and blue eyes. She is wearing a white petticoat, red stockings and black high-top shoes. She came with a wardrobe of five costumes with matching hats to be cut out. The dress in the upper left is bright pink trimmed with ecru lace and the hat is also pink with black feathers. The costume in the upper right is golden yellow trimmed with white lace and braid and blue bows. The hat is natural straw with blue ribbon and a big pink plume for trim. The golfing costume on the lower left has a red vest over a white blouse combined with a yellow and green plaid skirt. The matching hat is tan with a dark brown leather strap. The suit in lower center is a light brown jacket covering a white blouse and a blue skirt trimmed in dark blue. The matching straw hat has blue bows and black feathers. In the lower right a deep green coat accented with a fur collar and muff covers a rust dress. The matching hat is rust with a large dark green plume.

Illustration 168. 12½in (31.8cm) *Fanny Fairleigh* from the "Maidens Fair Series of Dressing Dolls" was published by R. Tuck and Sons Co. Ltd. "Art Publishers to their Majesties the King and Queen" (Edward and Alexandra) "London, Paris, Berlin, Toronto, Designed at the Studios in New York and Printed in Germany." The die-cut doll and clothes are in beautiful color. *Fanny Fairleigh* has blonde hair and blue eyes. She is wearing a white petticoat and camisole trimmed with blue ribbon and she is holding a pink rose. The dress on the left is white, trimmed with blue ribbon and accented with a corsage of blue flowers. Over her shoulder is a thin white shawl. The dress on the right is also white, decorated with blue embroidery. She is holding a bouquet of pink roses. (Two other outfits — one deep rose and the other dusty blue — are not pictured. Four hats are also not shown.) *McClelland Collection.*

Illustration 169. 12in (30.5cm), this unidentified young lady is marked only with letters on the tabs. She has blonde hair and blue eyes. She is wearing a white petticoat trimmed in blue and a matching blue hairbow. She has blue stockings and black shoes with pink bows. Costume C in the upper left is a rose colored coat trimmed with white fur and a white muff over a dark blue dress with gold trim. Costume B in the upper right is a light green nighty with pink roses trimmed with lace and pink ribbons. Costume D in the lower left is a pink dress with a green pattern. The insert in the neckline is white and the collar is blue, with a matching blue bow at the waist. The hat is pink and blue trimmed with red roses. Costume A in the lower right is a deep royal blue suit with a yellow, blue, red and green patterned vest and a pink sash, collar and cuffs. The matching hat is royal blue with a large brown plume.

MARY WARE DOLL BOOK

This unique paper doll book is hardbound with perforated pages. It has ten dolls and 38 costumes. Each page is printed in beautiful, soft colors. The paper dolls represent the characters from the very popular "Little Colonel Series" for young women written by Annie Fellows Johnston. The artwork was done by W. M. Crocker. The first printing of the book was in 1914.

RIGHT: Illustration 170. Mary Ware doll.

BELOW: LEFT TO RIGHT:
Illustration 171. Sailor dress and hat.

Illustration 172. Tan dress and hat.

Illustration 173. Middy blouse and skirt.

EASEL

If cut out and pasted on the back of the doll the figure can be made to stand.

Mary Ware

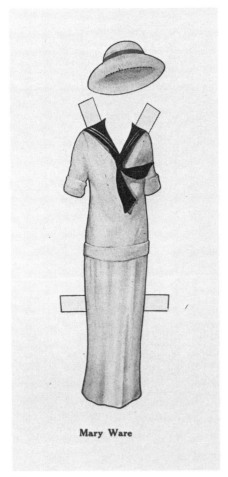

Mary Ware

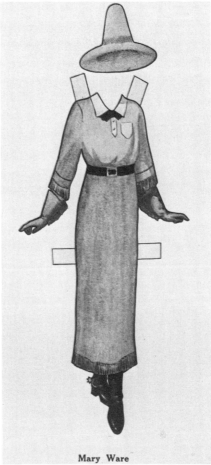

Mary Ware

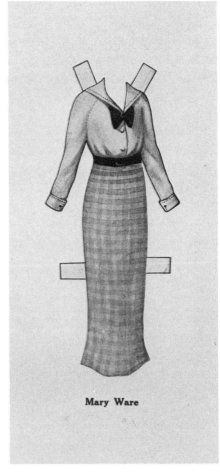

Mary Ware

82

Mary Ware

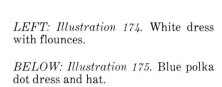

LEFT: *Illustration 174.* White dress with flounces.

BELOW: *Illustration 175.* Blue polka dot dress and hat.

RIGHT: *Illustration 176.* Pink dress.

Mary Ware

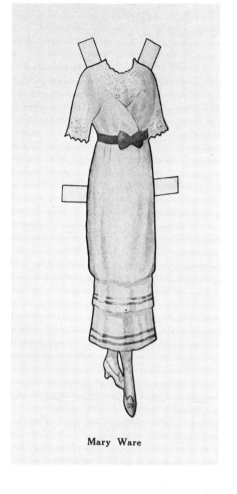

Mary Ware

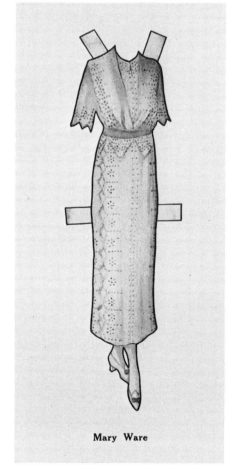

Mary Ware

LEFT: *Illustration 177.* White eyelet dress.

RIGHT: *Illustration 178.* Kimono robe.

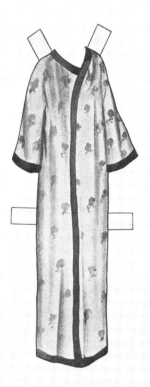

Mary Ware

CAROLYN CHESTER'S ROUND-BASE PAPER DOLLS GIVEN HISTORIC VALUE BY MR. CORWIN KNAPP LINSON, *printed in* The Delineator.

This series was published from January to June in 1913, showing 50 years of fashion change to commemorate the 15th anniversary of Butterick patterns. The artwork was done by Carolyn Chester, who was well-known for her three-dimensional paper dolls.

Illustration 179. May 1913, showing the fashions of 1903.

Illustration 180. June 1913, showing the current fashions.

Children of the Teens and Twenties

The 20th century brought with it many changes — social, industrial and political. There was increasing awareness of the importance of children as the modern concept of family was emerging. Children were becoming the center of family life.

In the previous century, society had been filled with many impoverished families, and childhood was a luxury that the lower classes could not afford for their children. These children were forced to work alongside their parents just to survive and were exposed to all aspects of adult life. Youngsters were often put into "service" working for wealthy families at very early ages. But, all of this was changing.

As industrialism increased, the middle class continued to grow. Social legislation was passed to protect children. Slowly, even children of the poorest families were allowed to enter the separate world of childhood. Laws began to require children to attend school. Children were forbidden to gamble, smoke or drink. Social legislation regulated children's work.

New jobs required more skilled and trained people, necessitating longer periods of education or apprenticeship. By World War I, most children were not emancipated until their late teens. These years of extended education led to the modern concept of adolescence.

Society began to accept the fact that children had their own rights. For the first time, they were able to grow up free to lead lives of their own choosing. They were no longer raised to be eternally indebted to their parents. Absolute parental authority no longer extended over a child's entire life.

Children now had a separate world, with its own fashions. They were no longer expected to look like miniature adults. New industrial advances and the ready-to-wear trade made mass produced clothing readily available. Such inventions as the knitting machine introduced new, more comfortable clothing to children. A greater variety of clothing in a wider selection of fabrics was also becoming available.

During the teens little girls began to wear dresses with longer waists and princess styles. The sleeve size decreased and emphasis moved to the shoulder with ruffles and cape collars. Pastel ribbon sashes were popular. It was fashionable for the hems of girls' skirts to show below their coats. High button shoes or black patent slippers with eyelets for bows were worn. The boys continued to wear the knickers and sailor suits but now wore them with knitted turtleneck sweaters. They wore either high tops or oxford shoes with laces. Boys wore their pants above the knee until the age of 16. With the invention of the rubber diaper cover little boys were permitted, for the first time, to wear trousers before they were toilet trained. The latest in sleep wear was pajamas.

Politically, clothing styles were greatly affected by World War I. Many of the materials were in short supply and much of the fabric went into military uniforms. Attitudes during these war years became very practical. While many of the men went off to the war, the women began to work in the factories and there was no time for extra ironing and starching and for the frivolous fashions so popular at the beginning of the century.

The twenties brought simpler styles and little girls' dresses became shorter; materials were softer and free-flowing. The natural waistline returned. Little boys wore long pants for the first time. Much of the clothing designed was influenced by the very popular art deco styles. The use of knitted underwear became wide spread. Denim coveralls, which were new at the turn of the century, continued to be popular. Rompers were fashionable for play. For the girls the silhouette was generally straighter and older girls dressed like their mothers in the flapper styles.

With this new period of childhood, parents felt the need for toys and books to entertain and instruct their children. Publishing companies were flourishing and new companies were being formed. The American Colortype Company was incorporated in 1902 as a consolidation of three smaller printing companies. Samuel Gabriel and Sons Company was founded in 1907. Other small printing companies included the Stecher Company of Rochester, New York, the Charles Thompson Company of Chicago, Illinois, Charles E. Graham of New York, and M. A. Donohue and Co. of Chicago, Illinois, all of which produced children's books and paper dolls during this time.

In the past few paper dolls were produced over ten inches tall, but during the teens and twenties bigger paper dolls became very popular. A series of paper dolls believed by many to be produced by the Woolworth Company were over 20in (50.8cm) tall.

Some of the first paper dolls produced by the Gabriel Company were *Dolly Dear, Dolly Delight* and *Dolly Darling*, each measuring 14in (35.6cm). One unidentified boy from Germany was also 14in (35.6cm) tall. The O. W. Nelson Company published several large dolls measuring over 20in (50.8cm) and some of these paper dolls were printed with advertising for the Minard's Company.

Advertising paper dolls continued to be a popular gimmick. They were often used to advertise children's clothes and patterns. *Bobby* and *Betty*, a pair of paper doll twins, appeared in the *Excella Pattern Book*. They wore clothes designed from Excella patterns. Miss Molly Munsing advertised knitted underwear for little girls. Elsie Dinsmore and her Little Sister advertised dresses which could be ordered through the mail by number.

The Elsie Dinsmore line of dresses was inspired by a popular character from a collection of books for young girls. Elsie Dinsmore was the heroine of an extensive series of Victorian novels written in England from 1867 to 1894. The author was Martha Findley, who wrote under the pen name of Farquharson. These popular stories were widely read in America during the first part of this century. Elsie was a poor little rich girl whose mother was dead. Her father traveled extensively on business and Elsie was forced to live with relatives. She was sweet and kind despite being treated cruelly by her cousins. Through many adversities she retained her angelic countenance and her great love for her father.

Deluxe paper dolls were still being imported from Europe for the more affluent children. Raphael Tuck & Sons and the J. W. Spear Company produced many of them. The Spear Company made some wonderful boxed sets in beautiful color, deeply embossed and some with interchangeable heads.

With people becoming more educated, one of the areas of great growth was the magazine industry. From the turn of the century many new magazines began to appear on the market. During the teens and into the twenties almost every ladies' magazine included paper doll and paper toy pages to entertain the children. The magazines often offered special paper doll sets as premiums for selling their subscriptions. Newspapers often ran paper dolls regularly for the children. These uncut pages are real treasures today because they were usually tossed out with the newspaper.

The paper dolls during this period were very realistic. Today they provide us with some of the best detailed records of the children's styles, the fabrics they chose and the ways that they combined them.

These years with their important social changes provide collectors with some of the wonderful and often hard-to-find treasures in their collections.

J. W. SPEAR COMPANY

The Spear Company was recognized in England for its parlor games, children's books and other paper toys and paper dolls. Like R. Tuck and Sons Limited, their paper dolls and other paper toys were designed in England but actually produced in Bavaria. Their early paper dolls date from the turn of the century and the company continued to produce deluxe paper dolls into the 1920s. Their symbol was a spear and shield marked "SPEAR SERIES."

Illustration 181. 10in (25.4cm) doll with four interchangeable heads from *Spear's Original Character Dolls* is dressed in a white petticoat trimmed with blue ribbons. The costume in the upper left is pink trimmed with white lace and green ribbons at the low waist. The matching hat is straw trimmed with pink roses and a big blue bow. The costume in the upper right is yellow with a white lace star collar. It has lace insertion threaded with blue ribbon at the waist and at the bottom of the sleeves. In the lower left is a green costume trimmed with dark red braid and a matching belt. The hat is straw with a dark red ribbon bow. The coat in the lower right is dark brown with a blue collar and cuffs edged with brown fur. The matching hat is brown with blue plumes. A Teddy Bear and other accessories are also included.

Illustration 182. 13in (33cm) Spear doll with five interchangeable heads. Some of these heads appeared in more than one set. *McClelland Collection.*

RIGHT: *Illustration 183.* Clothes for the Spear's doll include: in the upper left, a blue dress trimmed with a lavender insert down the front and a lavender collar and upper sleeves; the high neck and lower sleeves are white lace; her shoes and stockings are blue, and she wears white gloves and carries a metallic purse. In the upper right is her school costume, a brown jumper with a blue print blouse; she has a plain blue tie around the collar of the blouse; her gloves are brown and she is carrying a schoolbag. In the lower left, her coat is green trimmed with pink cuffs coordinated with a brown fur scarf and muff; pink bows on the fur muff match the cuffs; she is wearing dark blue stockings; white spats decorated with tiny blue buttons are worn over her black shoes. The dress in the lower right must be for a party; it is pink trimmed with pink ribbons and a bunch of violets at the bodice; she carries a fan in one hand and a dance card is attached to the other; she is wearing pink shoes and stockings. *McClelland Collection.*

ABOVE: *Illustration 184.* 7in (17.8cm) *Daisy and her Dresses* was produced by the Spear Company and printed with a matte finish. She is heavily embossed and the colors are dark but soft. This same set was reprinted at a later time in very bright colors on shiny paper.

Illustration 185. Daisy and her Dresses — box lid.

Illustration 186. 7in (17.8cm) *Peggy* from *Peggy and her new Outfit* has blonde hair and blue eyes. She wears a white petticoat trimmed with blue ribbon. Her wardrobe includes, in the upper left, a blue sweater over a white skirt trimmed with blue braid and a blue knit hat. In the upper right, a lavender jumper with a blue sash is over a white blouse with a ruffled collar and cuffs. The hat is straw with a blue band. In the lower left is a pink dress with ruffles on the skirt and trimmed with tiny white ruffles at the neck and at the bottom of the sleeves, it is belted with a wide white sash and combined with a straw hat decorated with big pink flowers. Her coat, on the lower right, is purple with a white fur collar and cuffs and has a matching fur muff. *Fertel Collection.*

Illustration 187. *Peggy and her new Outfit* — box lid. *Fertel Collection.*

89

LEFT: *Illustration 188.* 7in (17.8cm) *Joan* from *Joan and her new Frocks, Coats, Hats, Dolls and Toys* has blonde hair and blue eyes. She is wearing a white petticoat trimmed with blue ribbon. Her wardrobe includes, in the upper left, a white dress printed with pink roses and trimmed with blue binding and a blue ribbon belt. Her matching hat is blue with pink roses. In the upper right is a blue dress with white collar and cuffs and a black tie. With it is a straw hat decorated with a blue ribbon. Her coat, in the lower left, is red with gray fur trim and is combined with a matching red hat. In the lower right is a black and white check dress with a red bow at the neck and a matching red belt. Her hat is red with a black and white check bow. The set includes a doll, a duck and two buff colored toys presumably for the child to color.

**Note: *Joan* and *Peggy* were also printed in sheets to be cut out.

Illustration 189. Joan and her new Frocks, Coats, Hats, Dolls and Toys — box lid.

BIG DOLLS

During the teens and twenties big paper dolls — 14in (35.6cm) and taller — were popular. Some were for advertising but there is another group which remains somewhat of a mystery. The dolls, all over 20in (50.8cm) tall, were packaged in glassine envelopes that were very perishable, so what little information was on the envelopes is often lost. Dolls such as *Alice* and *Beatrice* seem to be from the same series. Some of them are marked with a "W" on the envelope which is believed to be associated with the F. W. Woolworth Co. There are over 20 different dolls in this group. Their envelopes have a code which seems to indicate that they were made from 1913 to 1918. Other dolls such as the unidentified one are wearing styles from the twenties and are made differently, indicating that they are probably from a different series. In addition, there are still more of these "big" dolls that are different from any of the ones pictured. They have varying numbers of costumes in their wardrobes, and many questions remain to be answered about them.

Illustration 190. 21in (53.3cm) *Alice*, from Set No. 1, is shown with her envelope, which gives no information about who printed her. It does state that the doll comes with three dresses and three hats and mentions that *Dorothy* is Set No. 2 and *Marion is Set No. 3. Alice* has light red hair and brown eyes. She is wearing a pink dress trimmed with red and white striped binding. Her hair bow is red and pink. Her shoes and stockings are white.

Illustration 191. Alice's clothes include: a white lace dress trimmed with a wide red sash and a matching white lace hat trimmed with red roses and a red bow on top; a blue coat trimmed with a wide white collar and cuffs, holding a tiny red purse and a straw hat edged with pink and decorated with a green bow; and a blue and white striped dress with blue collar and cuffs and blue buttons with a matching blue hat with a darker blue ribbon.

LEFT: *Illustration 192.* 21in (53.3cm) *Beatrice* from the "Fashion Dressing Doll" series is shown with her envelope. Marked "Set C," the envelope says that there are four sisters in the set — *Ethel, Helen, Beatrice* and *Lillian.* The only other information is a "W" in a diamond which is believed to stand for the Woolworth Company. *Beatrice* has black hair and brown eyes. She is wearing a pink dress trimmed with white at the neckline and at the edge of the sleeves, and a wide white band at the dropped waist. Her hair bow is pink with a narrow blue stripe. She is wearing white shoes and stockings.

Illustration 193. Beatrice's clothes include: a gold coat with a black ruffled collar and cuffs and a black band at the hem and a gold hat trimmed with blue and black ribbon; a red dress with wide, white braid down the front, around the hem and on the sleeves and a matching red hat trimmed with a white band and a big white bow on top; a blue dress decorated with wide white lace around a cape collar and down the front, a blue ribbon belt, coordinated with a white lace cap trimmed with a blue bow.

RIGHT: *Illustration 195.* 14¼in (36.3cm) boy marked only
"Germany." He is printed in rich color. He has brown hair and
blue eyes. His underwear is white; his shoes are white with
black toes and laces; his stockings are blue. He has two
costumes: (top) a two-piece suit in rust trimmed with black
buttons and a black belt and coordinated with a tan and rust
plaid cap; and (below) a green coat trimmed with an olive
collar and buttons over blue knee length pants and a white
shirt with a red tie; with it is a gray hat with a black band. A
walking stick, a soccer ball and a toy horse on wheels are also
included. The set came in a plain glassine envelope.

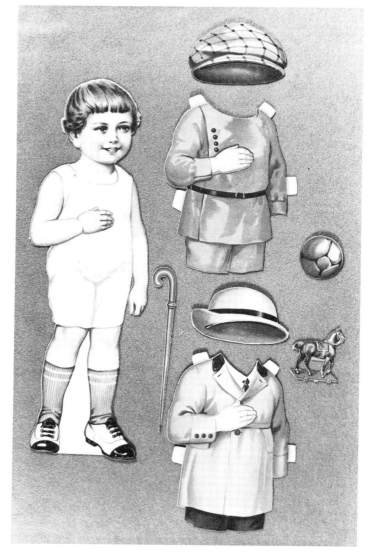

Illustration 194. 19½in (49.6cm) unidentified girl with brown
hair and blue eyes. She is wearing a dress with a green
windowpane plaid on white. Her shoes are white and her
socks are white with green and white stripes around the top.
She is standing on a green and yellow floor in front of a blue
planter. The dress in the upper left corner is light blue with
white, trimmed with blue embroidery at the neck, waist and
cuffs and a white hat with a lace ruffle and two blue bows; the
dress below it is dark green, red and blue plaid with a dark
blue bodice and a white blouse underneath and a natural
straw hat trimmed with blue ribbon; the coat on the right is
pink with light brown collar and cuffs and a pink hat with a
matching brown brim.

MINARD'S ADVERTISING DOLLS

The Minard's Liniment Company of Framingham, Massachusetts, offered several large paper dolls to promote their preparations. On the back of the dolls they claimed "Minard's Liniment was prescribed by Dr. Levi Minard in his private practice fifty years ago. An effective, economical and clean-to-use external application for rheumatism, neuralgia, pleurisy, stiff, twisted joints, sore, strained, or lame muscles, tired, aching feet, any pain or ache as well as for throat and lung troubles, and as a general family medicine." Each of the paper dolls holds a carton of the liniment which states "The Great Internal and External Remedy for Man and Beast." These dolls, with three complete costumes, were available for five - two cent stamps and the wrapper from a bottle of their liniment or their Hyliver Tablets. The dolls were copyright 1914, O. W. Nelson Company and printed by the American Lithographic Company of New York.

Illustration 196. 20½in (52.1cm) *Betty* has blonde hair, blue eyes and a blue bow in her hair. She is wearing a blue dress, white stockings and black and white high button shoes. Her extra costume has a navy blue jacket trimmed with red lapels and cuffs and gold buttons covering a white blouse and a red, navy and green plaid skirt. The matching hat is navy with a red, black and white plume.

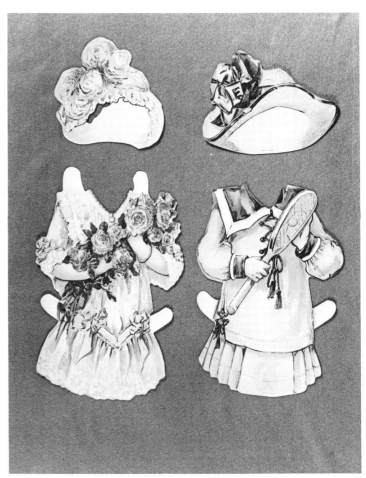

Illustration 197. Betty's dress on the left is white lace trimmed with blue ribbons. She is holding bright pink roses. The matching hat is also white lace trimmed with blue ribbon and a pink plume. The tennis outfit on the right is pale gold with a brown collar and cuffs edged in white. The matching hat is gold straw trimmed with brown ribbon.

LEFT: Illustration 198. 20½in (52.1cm) *Olive* has brown hair and brown eyes. She has a big pink bow in her hair. She is wearing a pink long-waisted dress trimmed with white lace and white insertion, and her shoes and stockings are also white. The extra costume is a deep purple coat with a wide white lace collar and lace cuffs covering a white dress. She is holding a red rose in one hand and a gold purse in the other. The coordinated hat is deep purple trimmed with pink ribbon and a pink plume.

Illustration 199. Olive's sailor dress is white trimmed with a blue collar and cuffs and blue cording. She is holding a shovel and pail. The matching sailor hat is white with blue trim. The dress on the right is a red and white print fabric trimmed with red at the neckline, down the sleeves and around the low waist. She is holding an apple and a jump rope. The hat for this outfit, which is not shown, is of straw trimmed in red.

SAMUEL GABRIEL & SONS

The Samuel Gabriel and Sons Company was founded in 1907 in New York. Their trademark was a palette and brush with the capital letter "G" within. They published children's books, postcards, games, valentines and paper dolls. The company was known for the quality of its products. They did excellent quality printing in deep, rich colors. They began producing paper dolls in 1911. The early Gabriel paper dolls were often printed in Germany. Many of the paper dolls were elaborate and came as deluxe boxed sets. The company made a number of paper dolls and valentines with moving eyes. Later the American Colortype Company did much of their printing. Samuel Gabriel died in 1920 but his two sons continued in the business. In the 1930s, during the depression, the Gabriel Company joined with the American Colortype Company. Today the company, is part of Gabriel Industries, is among the top ten manufacturers of toys in America. Gabriel Industries is a diversified manufacturer of toys, sporting goods, office furniture and home playground equipment.

Illustration 200. 14in (35.6cm) *Dolly Dear* #1 has blonde hair and blue eyes. She is wearing a white petticoat trimmed with blue ribbon and black shoes and stockings. The coat on the far left is dark green trimmed with brown fur; the hat is green with a rust colored bow. The shoes and stockings are brown. Next is a pink gown with pink roses attached to white veiling. To the right of the doll is a bright blue swimsuit trimmed with white braid and a blue and white bandana is tied for her head. On the far right is a coat of white fur with a matching hat and white leggings. This doll dates from 1911 and she is one of the earliest Gabriel paper dolls.

OPPOSITE PAGE TOP: Illustration 201. 14in (35.6cm) *Dolly Delight #2* has light brown hair and brown eyes. She is wearing a white petticoat and white high button shoes. The outfit on the far left is a white sailor dress trimmed in red. Her hat is natural straw edged in brown and her shoes and stockings are red. Next is a print dress with pink and green flowers on a white background accented with green bows on the shoulders and a green sash. The straw hat is trimmed with green ribbon and pink flowers, and the shoes and stockings are green. Her coat is pink trimmed with a white lace collar and cuffs, and white leggings, and the hat is pink with pink ribbon and a pink plume. The dress on the far right is blue and white check with a white blouse. The white eyelet hat is trimmed with blue ribbon and she has brown shoes and stockings. Another of the early Gabriel paper dolls, *Dolly Delight* is from the same series as *Dolly Dear*.

Illustration 202. 14in (35.6cm) *Dolly Darling #3* has dark brown hair and blue eyes. She is wearing a white petticoat and black shoes and stockings. On the far left is a white dress trimmed with bright pink ribbons down the front and a bright pink sash; she has a matching pink ribbon for her hair. Next is a dress of gold trimmed with brown braid and a brown sash over a white blouse; her hat is gold edged in brown and decorated with orange flowers. The dress to the right of the doll is red dots on white and is banded in red; the matching hat is straw trimmed with red cherries and edged in black with a big black bow. The coat on the far right is also red, trimmed with black fur and the matching hat is black fur with a red crown. The doll is also another early Gabriel paper doll dating from 1911 and from the same series.

Illustration 203. "The Darling" Series of New Dressing Dolls, No. 11, *Darling Daisy and her Dresses and Hats* — box lid marked "Published by Saml. Gabriel Sons & Company, N.Y. "Printed in Germany." *McClelland Collection.*

Illustration 204. 9in (22.9cm) *Darling Daisy* has brown hair and blue eyes. She came with four outfits. *McClelland Collection.*

Illustration 206. *The Ever-New Doll* came with four inter-changeable heads and she had hinged arms. *McClelland Collection.*

ABOVE: Illustration 205. The Ever-New Doll — box lid marked "No.D 115 Sam'l Gabriel & Sons & Company, New York." *McClelland Collection.*

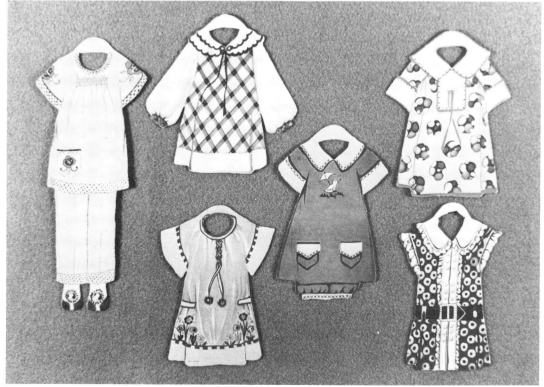

Illustration 207. *The Ever-New Doll* came with six brightly colored outfits. *McClelland Collection.*

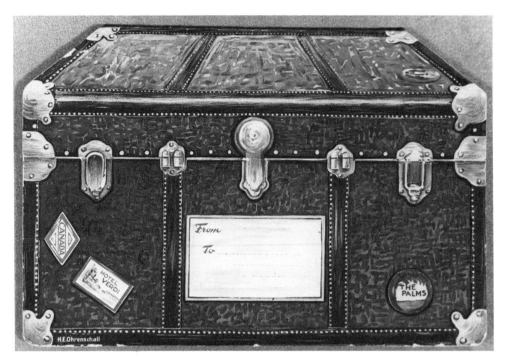

Illustration 208. Betty is Going Away to Boarding School. The folder, which looks like a trunk, folds out to reveal *Betty* and her wardrobe.

BELOW: Illustration 209. Betty is Going Away to Boarding School was designed to encourage a child to create lots of original costumes for *Betty* in addition to the ones included in the folder.

Illustration 210. 9in (22.9cm) *Susan* has blue eyes that move when her pink hair bow is moved from side to side. The doll was die-cut and came and in a glassine envelope with three costumes to be cut out. Her stand is marked "Susan, Printed in Germany," and "US patent Oct.21. 1919." The "Play Dress" on the right is bright pink trimmed in a darker pink.

Illustration 211. Susan's "Party Dress" is white with blue polka dots and blue trim at the neck, sleeves and waist. Her matching hat is white with a blue polka dot band and bow. Her "Walking Suit" is blue trimmed with white fur and a white muff and leggings. The hat is also blue with white fur trim.

DOLLY SHEETS — D100

This Gabriel book of paper dolls was copyrighted 1922. It contained four pages of paper dolls to cut out. Each doll had four costumes with matching hats. These same dolls also came individually packaged in envelopes. The tabs of the pieces were marked with the name of the doll that they fit and with a letter and number. The letter represented the doll; for instance, *Grace* was "A." All of *Grace's* clothes were marked with an "A." Her costumes and hats were A1 through A4. The number was for the number of the costume and its matching hat. Because the doll's letters are not consecutive, there are undoubtedly other dolls in this series and possibly other combinations of dolls in other books of "Dolly Sheets." This book, with pages of lightweight cardboard, was printed in the United States.

Illustration 212. "Dolly Sheets" — cover.

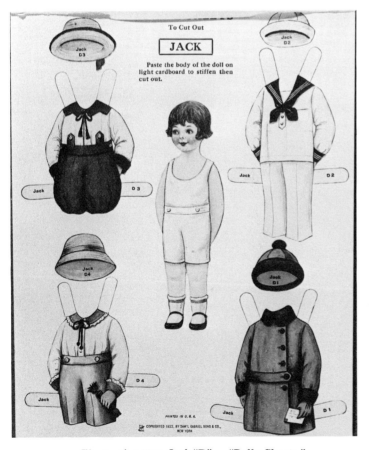

Illustration 213. Jack "D" — "Dolly Sheets."

Illustration 214. Ruth "F" — "Dolly Sheets."

102

Illustration 215. Grace "A" — "Dolly Sheets."

Illustration 216. Nancy "E" — "Dolly Sheets."

103

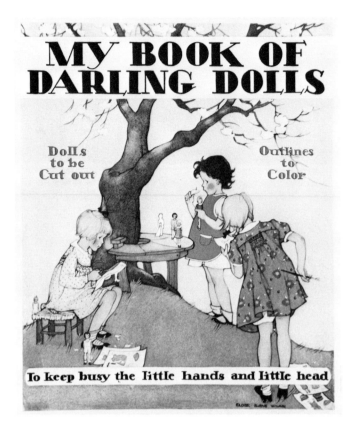

My Book of Darling Dolls was illustrated by Eloise Burns Wilken for the Gabriel Company. The book features one page of clothes that are beautifully printed in full color and an identical page which has outlines for the child to color in. The tabs of the outfits are marked with the name of the doll that they fit. The book was printed in the United States.

Illustration 217. My Book of Darling Dolls —cover.

Illustration 218. Nancy's & Barbara's Clothes, My Book of Darling Dolls.

Illustration 219. Sally's & Betty's Clothes, My Book of Darling Dolls.

SALLY'S & BETTY'S CLOTHES

Play dress and hat

Jockey cap for Sally

Winter coat and hat

Betty's flower girl dress

Riding habit

Everyday dress

Sunday dress

Illustration 219. Sally's & Betty's Clothes, My Book of Darling Dolls.

SALLY'S & BILLY'S CLOTHES

Winter costume

Billy's Scotch costume and hat

Overcoat and hat

Party suit

Sunday dress

School suit

Summer costume

Illustration 220. Sally's & Billy's Clothes, My Book of Darling Dolls.

Illustration 221. *Pattie's & Nancy's Clothes, My Book of Darling Dolls.*

Illustration 223. *Sylvia and Her Seven Frocks* appeared in *The Designer* magazine in October 1917. This was one of a series of paper doll pages that appeared in 1917 and 1918 about Sylvia and other children drawn by Bell Colborne. *The Designer* was published from 1898 until 1920 when it joined *The Delineator. McClelland Collection.*

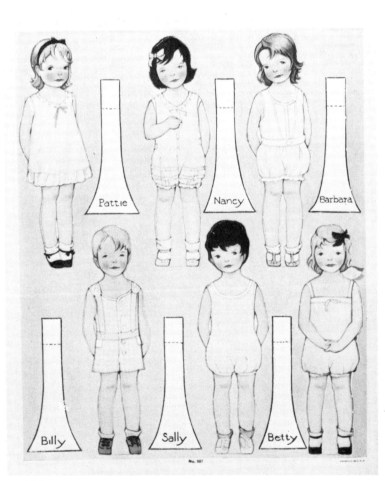

LEFT: *Illustration 222.* Back cover — the dolls are die-cut; *My Book of Darling Dolls.*

Illustration 224. Betty and Bobby, the Excella Twins, appeared in the *Excella Fashion Book* during the twenties. Advertising said that they would appear in every issue. Their outfits were available in printed patterns for children from ages one to twelve.

Illustration 225. This ad for the *Excella Twins* was probably handed out at pattern counters.

MUNSINGWEAR ADVERTISING DOLLS

With the introduction of the knitting machine, knitted underwear became popular because it was so light weight, warm and comfortable. The Munsingwear Company was a major producer of knitted underwear for adults and children. At one time the company employed more than 3500 people in their factory in Minneapolis, Minnesota. These paper dolls were provided by the company to local stores to distribute. Each store could have their own name and address printed at the top.

Illustration 226. This uncut sheet of *Miss Molly Munsing* and her wardrobe of eight costumes and accessories is bordered in green. *McClelland Collection.*

Illustration 227. This uncut sheet of *Miss Molly Munsing* and her wardrobe of eight costumes and accessories is bordered in tan.

ELSIE DINSMORE

Elsie Dinsmore and her Little Sister advertised dresses for stores that carried their dresses. The dresses were budget priced and could be ordered by number. They came in a variety of colors and sizes. The paper dolls and their dresses came printed in folders which opened out with complete descriptions of each garment on the back. These folders were available to the stores, which could have their own name printed on the back. Stores that offered the paper dolls included: The Basement Store of the Wm. H. Block Co., Indianapolis, Indiana; Magnus Myers of Chicago, Illinois; A. C. Haslanger of Mishawaka, Indiana; L. Bischof of Crawfordsville, Indiana; and Grieve and Walker of Mendota, Illinois. The dresses were mostly made of cotton. Stripes, checks and plaid patterns were popular. The dresses featured smocking, embroidery and buttons for decoration.

Illustration 228. 7in (17.8cm) *Little Sister* and 7½in (19.1cm) *Elsie* are from the advertising set *Elsie Dinsmore and Little Sister Dolls.* They came in an envelope from Magnus Myers of Chicago. The outfits are numbered: left to right - #1520, #1612, #1616; row 2 - #1510, #1639, #1615, #1638; row 3 - #1537, #1514, #1602, #1645; row 4 - #1523, #1511, #1640, #1623. *McClelland Collection.*

Illustration 229. 6½in (16.5cm) *Elsie Dinsmore* and her costumes numbered: left to right - #840, #849, #857; row 2 -#858, #828; row 3 - #830, #831; row 4 - #847, #843, #854. *McClelland Collection.*

RIGHT: *Illustration 230.* 7in (17.8cm) *Little Sister* and her costumes numbered: left to right - #111, #167; row 2 - #156, #147; row 3 - #144, #157; row 4 - #158, #161, #114. *McClelland Collection.*

Continued on page 127.

110

Color Illustration 1. Die Schwestern, a boxed set printed in Germany. McClelland Collection.

ABOVE: Color Illustration 2. Our Treasure by Raphael Tuck. McClelland Collection.

Color Illustration 3. Bridal Party from the Raphael Tuck "Bridal Party Series of Dressing Dolls." From the combined collections of Cynthia Musser and Joyce McClelland.

Color Illustration 4. Dolls' Wedding Series produced by Clark's ONT Thread. *From the combined collections of Janie Barrett and Cynthia Musser.*

BELOW: Color Illustration 5. Victorian gentleman printed in Germany.

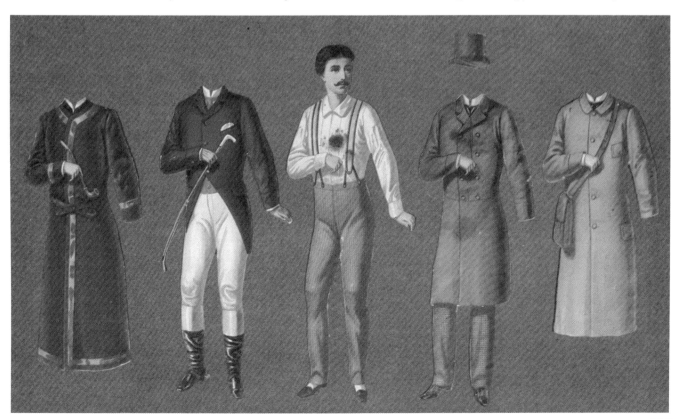

Color Illustration 6. Hood's Family. McClelland Collection.

BELOW: Color Illustration 7. Costumes for the *Hood's Family. McClelland Collection.*

Color Illustration 8. Minnie Miller printed by McLoughlin Brothers.

BELOW: Color Illustration 9. Myra Mild printed by McLoughlin Brothers.

CLOCKWISE:
Color Illustration 10. Susie from Susie's Pets printed by McLoughlin Brothers. McClelland Collection.

Color Illustration 11. Edith advertised for Dr. Miles.

Color Illustration 12. Unidentified boy printed in Germany in the teens.

OPPOSITE PAGE: Color Illustration 13. Children at the Beach, printed in Germany. McClelland Collection.

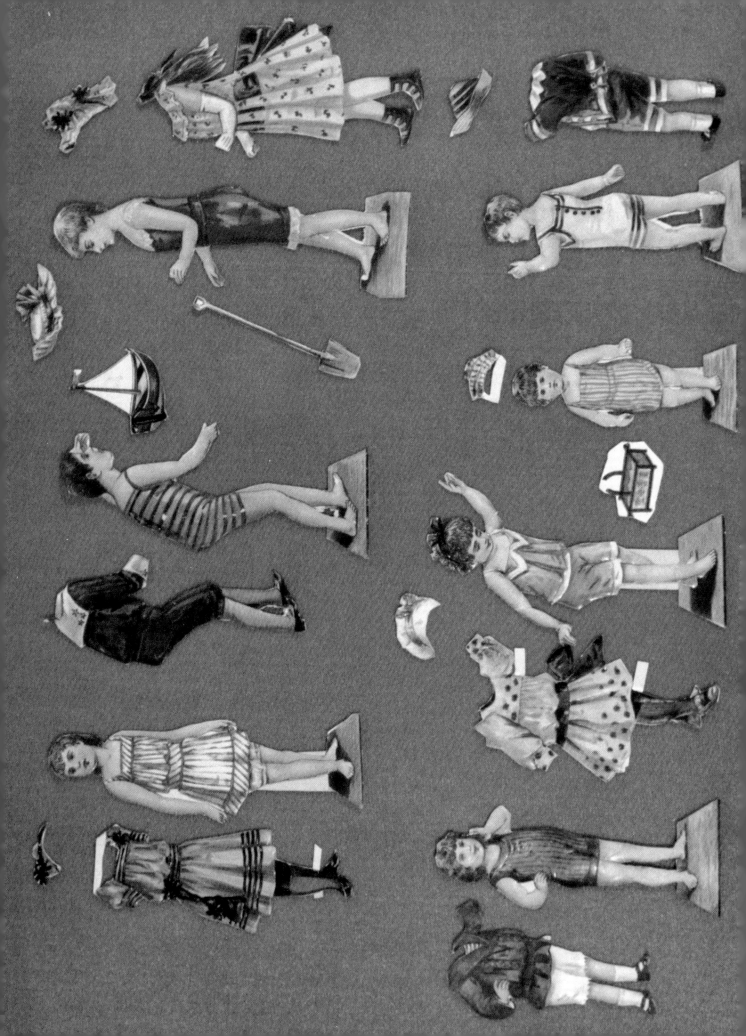

Color Illustration 14. Grand-mother's Tea Party produced by the A&P Tea Company.

Color Illustration 15. Bobby and Betty, The Excella Twins, from the *Excella Pattern Book.*

Color Illustration 16. J. W. Spear paper doll with interchangeable heads.

Color Illustration 17. Polly's Brother Percy from "Polly's Paper Playmates."

Color Illustration 18. The *African Series* offered by the National Candy Company.

LEFT: Color Illustration 19. Teddy Bear Paper Doll published by Selchow and Righter.

OPPOSITE PAGE: TOP: Color Illustration 20. Chubby Cubby printed by the American Colortype Company. *McClelland Collection.*

BOTTOM LEFT: Color Illustration 21. Pretty Kitty and *Dandy Doggie* printed by the American Colortype Company.

BOTTOM RIGHT: Color Illustration 22. The Mousie Bride drawn by Grace G. Drayton and printed in *Pictorial Review.*

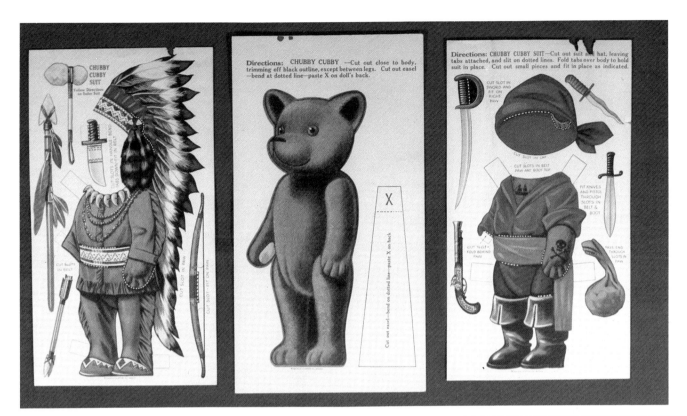

Directions: CHUBBY CUBBY ---Cut out close to body, trimming off black outline, except between legs. Cut out easel ---bend at dotted line---paste X on doll's back.

Directions: CHUBBY CUBBY SUIT---Cut out suit and hat, leaving tabs attached, and slit on dotted lines. Fold tabs over body to hold suit in place. Cut out small pieces and fit in place as indicated.

THE MOUSIE BRIDE
From the Nursery Rime, "Froggie Would Awooing Go"
Ninth in the New Series of Cut-out Pictures: By Grace G. Drayton

ABOVE: *Color Illustration 23.* Rose O'Neill's *Kewpies with Ragsy and Ritzy Cut-Out Dolls* published by the Whitman Company and copyright Rose O'Neill.

Color Illustration 24. Scootles and Kewpie Doll Book illustrated by Rose O'Neill and published by the Saalfield Company. *McClelland Collection.*

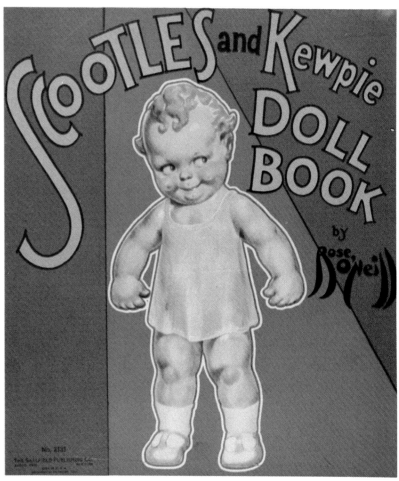

Color Illustration 25. Dolly and Lottie, a post card paper doll illustrated by Margaret G. Hays.

BELOW: Color Illustration 26. Unidentified Brownie.

OPPOSITE PAGE: Color Illustration 27. *Kaiserin Und Prinzesschen*, a wonderful boxed set printed in Germany. *McClelland Collection.*

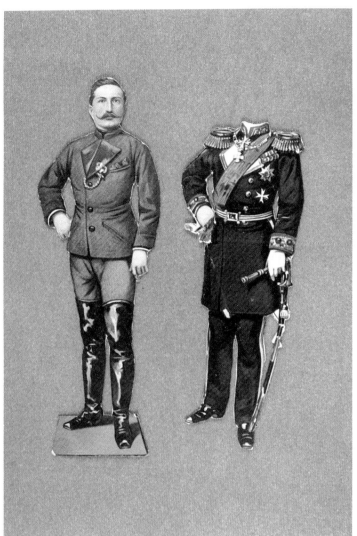

Color Illustration 28. Kaiser Wilhelm II of Prussia printed in Germany. *McClelland Collection.*

Color Illustration 29. Irene of Hesse, printed in Germany.

Color Illustration 30. The Marquis and Marchioness published by McLoughlin Brothers.

BELOW: Color Illustration 31. Queen Elizabeth from E. S. Tucker's Famous Queens and Martha Washington, published by the Stokes Company.

Continued from page 110.

Illustration 231. 7½in (19.1cm) *Elise Dinsmore* and her costumes numbered: left to right - #627, #600, #646; row 2 - #642, #610; row 3 - #607, #625; row 4 - #624, #605, #608. *McClelland Collection.*

Illustration 232. 7¼in (18.3cm) *Elsie Dinsmore* and her costumes numbered: left to right - #200, #202, #213; row 2 - #225, #246; row 3 - #234, #235; row 4 - #236, #243, #247.

Illustration 233. 7in (17.8cm) *Little Sister* and her costumes numbered: left to right - #170, #173, #120; row 2 - #157, #164; row 3 - #112, #103; row 4 - #172, #148, #169.

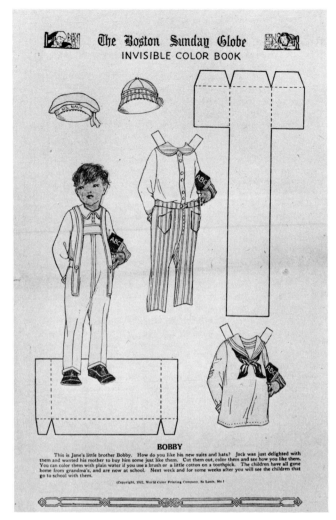

Illustration 234. This uncut sheet of *Bobby* and his clothes was part of a series that appeared in *The Boston Sunday Globe.* It is copyright 1922, World Color Printing Company, St, Louis, Missouri. It probably appeared in other newspapers as well. These pages were designed to be colored and cut out. *McClelland Collection.*

AMERICAN COLORTYPE COMPANY

The American Colortype Company was incorporated in Clifton, New Jersey, on February 21, 1902. It was the consolidation of the Osborne Company of Newark, New Jersey, the American Three-Color Company and National Colortype Company. The Osborne Company manufactured advertising calendars and the other two companies were known for their work with color photography for commercial reproductions. The company had a reputa-

tion for high grade color work. In 1957, the American Colortype Company merged with the Rapid Electro-Type Company to become the Rapid American Corporation. The company produced beautiful, high quality paper dolls during the teens and twenties. Some of these paper dolls were used for advertising premiums and as prizes for selling magazine subscriptions.

PATRIOTIC DRESSING DOLLS

Influenced by World War I, many paper dolls had military uniforms in their wardrobe. The American Colortype Company produced this set, *The Patriotic Dressing Dolls,* for *Farm and Home* magazine as a prize for selling magazine subscriptions.

The company also printed these same dolls in a larger size and sold them separately in envelopes. The set consists of two dolls, a boy and a girl, each with five outfits to be cut out. However, the dolls that appear in these sets vary.

TOP TO BOTTOM:
Illustration 235. The Patriotic Dressing Dolls — Laurette No. 609, envelope, *David,* No. 612.

Illustration 236. Laurette's clothes: No. 903, Miss Liberty; No. 904, Red Cross Nurse; No. 906, Miss Patriot; No. 907, Glory on Parade; No. 908, Miss Knitting.

Illustration 237. David's clothes: No. 823, Boy Scout; No. 847, Soldier; No. 900, Our Jackie; No. 901, Colonial Drummer; No. 902, Our Sammy.

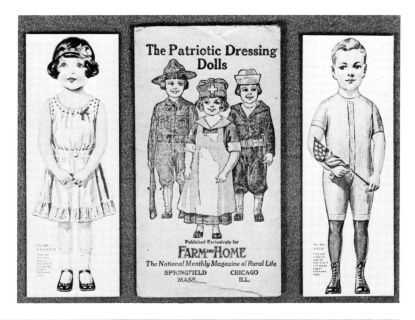

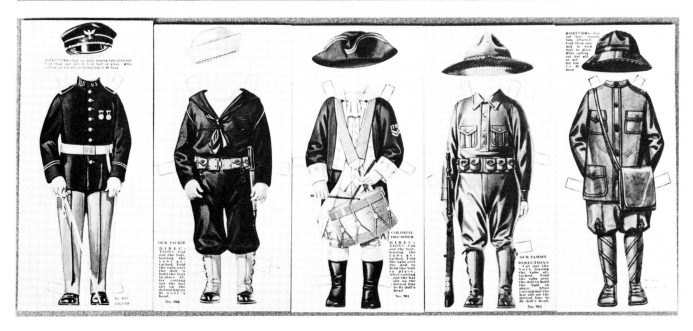

Favorite Families

Families have always been a favorite topic for paper dolls. In bygone years the extended family was an important part of everyday life, with grandparents, aunts, uncles and cousins all living nearby. Children found security and roots through these close associations. They enjoyed all sorts of family activities and could re-enact these happy experiences with their paper families. These paper dolls remind us of a time when families were larger and more interdependent. When the family reunion was an annual event, when riding in an automobile to Grandmother's was something special, and live-in servants were like members of the family.

Magazines that published monthly pages of paper dolls frequently used the family theme to keep children looking for the next issue. One of the earliest and largest families to appear in the magazines was the "Lettie Lane Family" which began in *The Ladies' Home Journal* in October of 1908 and appeared monthly until June of 1911. The artwork for this family was done by Sheila Young.

The series included a beautiful wedding for *Lettie's* sister and later a series of Around-the-World pages featuring paper dolls of foreign children. The first pages were so popular that in 1909, George W. Jacobs and Company of Philadelphia, Pennsylvania, reprinted some of them and packaged them in folders that looked like brick houses. They were marked "The Lettie Lane Paper Family." In 1915, Sheila Young did a second series for *The Ladies' Home Journal*, which introduced the *Betty Bonnet* family and friends month after month. It continued until 1918.

After Lettie Lane, other magazines followed with their family series. In 1912, *The Delineator* published *Adele* and her little sister by Carolyn Chester. In 1913 *The Woman's Magazine* printed the "Jointed Paper Doll Family," also by Carolyn Chester. The same year *The Delineator* introduced the "Margaret Butterick" series with unique dolls that had eyes which opened and closed.

McCall's Magazine is best known for its "Betsy McCall" series, which began in the fifties and continues today. However, as early as 1910 it printed *Dolly Dolliver*, her brother and *Baby Dolliver*. In the twenties it printed the well-known *Honti Family*. *Pictorial Review* introduced *Dolly Dingle* and her family and friends in the teens. This series turned out to be very successful, and ran regularly for 17 years (see Chapter 8). The list goes on and on.

Newspaper supplements produced paper dolls and paper toys about a number of different topics. They did many features for the little boys, but they produced a beautiful series called "Polly's Paper Playmates" for the little girls in 1910-1911. This series ran weekly for 24 weeks. *Polly* with her brothers, sisters and cousins displayed clothes for all sorts of activities.

Advertisers also produced paper families to promote their products. *The Hood's Family* promoted patent medicine in the 1890s (See Chapter 2). *The Munsingwear Family* was printed in the 1920s to advertise the latest in knit underwear for the entire family. *The Munsingwear Family* was offered in one long strip with eight family members all shown in their underwear.

By the thirties, publishers were producing many wonderful families as boxed sets and in book form. One of the most delightful boxed sets was done by the Samuel Gabriel and Sons Company. *The Winkle Family* is made up of seven dolls with clothing to be cut out. Cleverly, their box is a picture of their house. The dolls are softly colored and have whimsical character faces. Also during the thirties, the Whitman Company produced memorable families such as *Family of Paper Dolls* (#991) drawn by Queen Holden; and Saalfield published *The Walking Paper Family* (#1074, 1934), and *Paper Doll Family* (#2109, 1935). These were all in book form.

POLLY'S PAPER PLAYMATES

These beautiful sheets were printed in full color by the Gray Lithograph Company of New York. They appeared as newspaper supplements in the following newspapers: *The Baltimore American, The Boston Post, The New York Sunday American* and *The Public Ledger.*

Illustration 238. Polly's Playtime, October 2, 1910. Kaufman Collection.

Illustration 239. Polly's Schooldays, October 9, 1910. Kaufman Collection.

Illustration 240. Polly's Brother Percy, October 16, 1910.

Illustration 241. Polly's Cousin Janet, October 23, 1910. *Kaufman Collection.*

Illustration 242. Polly's Brother at School, October 30, 1910. *Fertel Collection.*

Illustration 243. Polly's Cousin Janet at the Seashore, November 6, 1910.

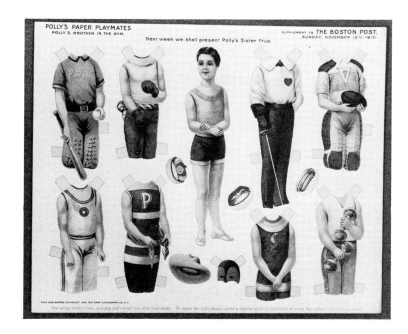

Illustration 244. Polly's Brother in the Gym, November 13, 1910.

Illustration 245. Polly's Sister Prue, November 20, 1910. *Kaufman Collection.*

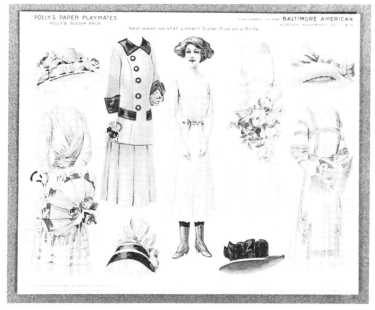

Illustration 246. Sister Prue as a Bride, November 27, 1910. *McClelland Collection.*

133

Illustration 247. Sister Prue's Young Man, December 4, 1910. Kaufman Collection.

Illustration 248. The Bridesmaid, December 11, 1910. McClelland Collection.

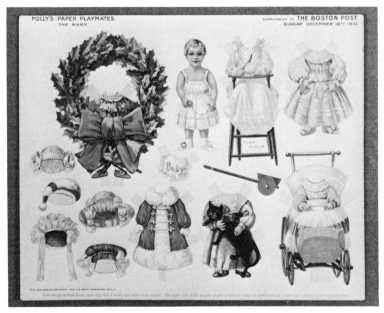

Illustration 249. The Baby, December 18, 1910. McClelland Collection.

Illustration 250. Cousin Janet at a Christmas Party, December 25, 1910. *Kaufman Collection.*

Illustration 251. Sister Prue on Commonwealth Avenue, January 1, 1911. *McClelland Collection.*

Illustration 252. Sister Prue at the Opera, January 8, 1911. *Fertel Collection.*

Illustration 253. Cousin Janet at the Horse Show,
January 15, 1911. Fertel Collection.

Illustration 254. Cousin Janet at the Rink, *January*
22, 1911. McClelland Collection.

Illustration 255. Sister Prue at the Costume Ball,
January 29, 1911. Fertel Collection.

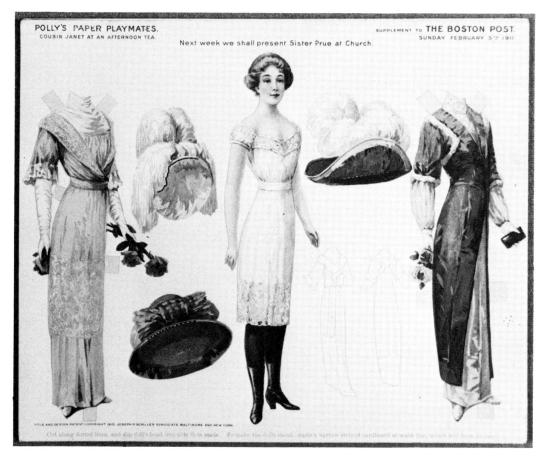

Illustration 256. Cousin Janet at an Afternoon Tea, February 5, 1911. McClelland Collection.

Illustration 257. Sister Prue at Church, February 12, 1911. Kaufman Collection.

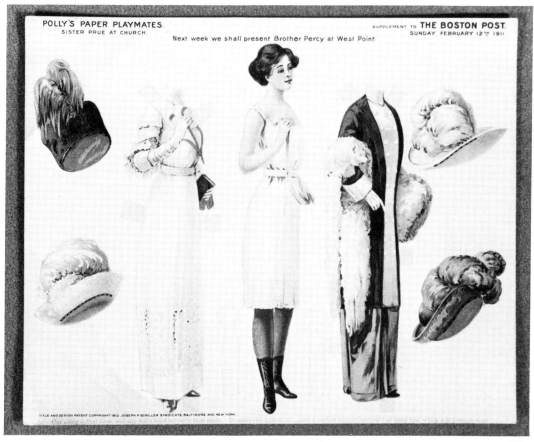

Illustration 258. **Brother Percy at West Point,** *February 19, 1911. Fertel Collection.*

Illustration 259. **Cousin Janet's Calling Day,** *February 26, 1911. Kaufman Collection.*

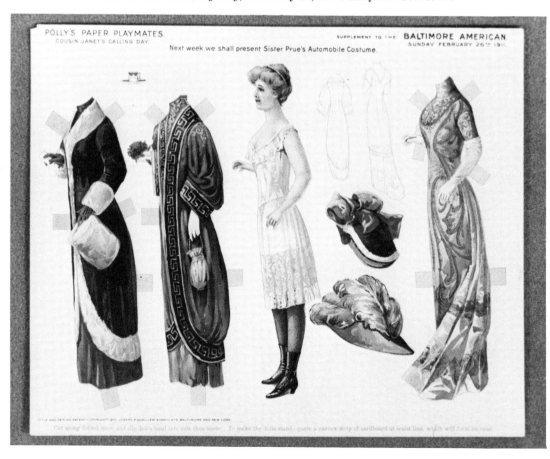

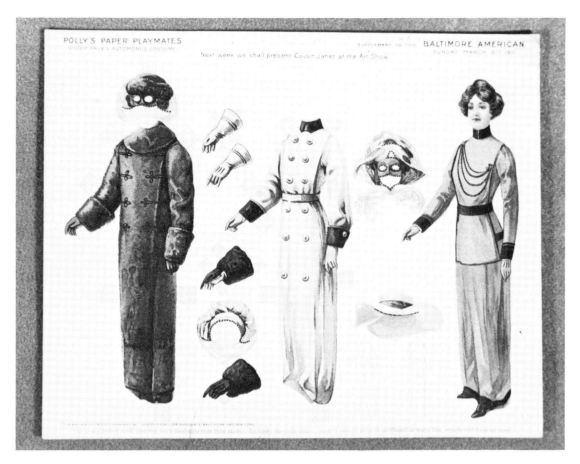

Illustration 260. Sister Prue's Automobile Costume, **March 5, 1911.** *Kaufman Collection.*

Illustration 261. Cousin Janet at the Art Show, **March 12, 1911.** *Fertel Collection.*

THE MUNSINGWEAR FAMILY CUTOUTS

This family of eight came in a long folder advertising that Munsingwear had underwear for every member of the family. *McClelland Collection.*

Illustration 262. Grandfather, Grandmother, Father and *Mother* — each has one extra outfit and hat.

Illustration 263. Older Brother, Younger Brother, Older Sister and *Younger Sister* — each has two extra outfits and hats.

Illustration 264. This advertising appeared on the back of the folder.

JOINTED PAPER DOLL FAMILY

This unusual family of paper dolls appeared in
The Woman's Magazine during 1913. The series,
drawn by Carolyn Chester, was an example of the
three-dimensional paper dolls for which she became
very well known. Many of her paper dolls appeared
in the *The Delineator* magazine.

*Illustration 265.
Jean — Our Jointed
Paper Doll,* March
1913. *McClelland
Collection.*

*Illustration 266. The Jointed Paper-Doll Family, April 1913.
McClelland Collection.*

*Illustration 267. Katie of the Jointed Paper-Doll Family,
June 1913. McClelland Collection.*

Illustration 268. *Two More Members of Our Jointed Paper-Doll Family, IV - Baby Polly and her Irish Nurse, Norah, July 1913. McClelland Collection.*

Illustration 269. *The Jointed Paper-Doll Family, V - At the Seashore with Katie's Big Sister, Mary Louise, September 1913.*

THE BUTTERICK FAMILY

This series appeared in *The Delineator* magazine in 1913 and 1914. It was drawn by Ella Dolbear Lee. These paper dolls were very cleverly designed with many three-dimensional effects. They were so unique that the magazine even applied for a patent for them.

The dolls are front and back when put together. Their clothes are all wrap-around and the dolls even have moving eyes. Many of the accessories add to the three-dimensional effect, for example an umbrella that is open over the doll's shoulder.

Illustration 270. Margaret Butterick - The Cut-Out Doll That Opens and Shuts Her Eyes, July 1913 — the first of the series.

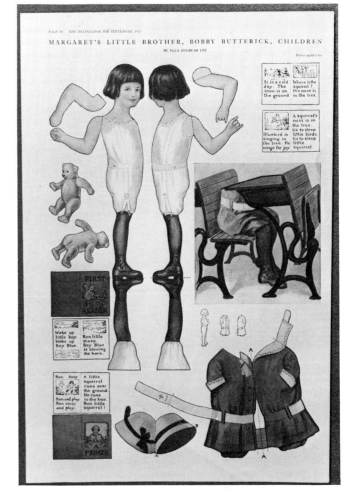

Illustration 271. Margaret's Little Brother, Bobby Butterick, Children, September 1913 — the second of the series.

144

Illustration 272. Margaret Butterick's Little Sister Betty and Her Doll, Bettina, October 1913 — the third of the series. (In November a page entitled "The Bedroom at Grandmother's" appeared which featured a bed that the dolls could slip into, but no doll was included.)

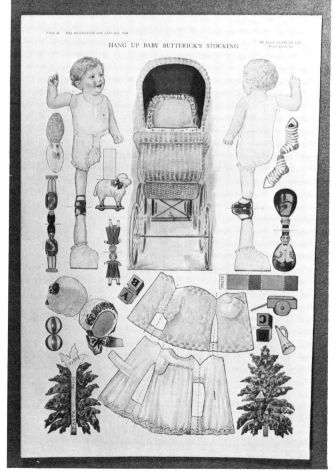

Illustration 273. Hang Up Baby Butterick's Stocking, January 1914. (In February 1914, a page entitled "When Your Butterick Paper Dolls Have Dinner" appeared but there were no dolls. This was the end of the series.)

THE LETTIE LANE PAPER FAMILY

"The Lettie Lane Paper Family" drawn by Sheila Young appeared first in *The Ladies' Home Journal* beginning in 1908. The next year George W. Jacobs and Company began reprinting a number of these pages and packaged them in folders that looked like brick houses. The houses came in different colors —brick red, orange, yellow and blue. Some of the folders contained six sheets and others only four which were printed in one continuous folded page. It is uncertain which sheets came in which folder and it is likely that the choice of sheets varied since many companies mixed things to keep up interest.

Illustration 274. "The Lettie Lane Paper Family" — orange folder, first series.

Illustration 275. The Lettie Lane Paper Family. (First of the series, appeared in *The Ladies' Home Journal* October 1908.)

Illustration 276. Presenting Lettie's Grandmother, Who Brings Christmas Presents to Lettie (appeared in *The Ladies' Home Journal*, December 1908).

Illustration 277. Presenting Lettie's Baby Sister, with Her Nurse and Some of Her Belongings (appeared in *The Ladies' Home Journal*, January 1909).

Illustration 278. Presenting Lettie's Sister as a Bride (appeared in *The Ladies' Home Journal*, March 1909).

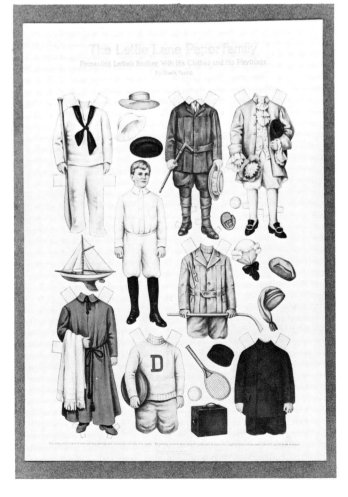

Illustration 279. Presenting Lettie's Brother, with His Clothes and His Playthings (appeared in *The Ladies' Home Journal*, June 1909).

148

The Lettie Lane Paper Family

Presenting One of Lettie's Dolls, With Her Hats and Dresses

By Sheila Young

Illustration 280. Presenting One of Lettie's Dolls, With Her Hats and Dresses (appeared in *The Ladies' Home Journal*, July 1909.)

Illustration 281. The Winkle Family (D127) published by the Samuel Gabriel Sons & Company of New York — folder showing the Winkle House (Gabriel Industries, Inc., a division of CBS, Inc.). *McClelland Collection.*

Illustration 282. The Winkle Family. McClelland Collection.

Illustration 283. Clothes for the *Winkle Family. McClelland Collection.*

Bears and Such . . .

Chapter 7

Children have always been fascinated with animals, especially Teddy Bears. Quickly these appealing creatures are made into toys that take on human qualities and soon begin to sport hats, jackets, bonnets, dresses and hairbows. Just as with other toys, these appealing characters have been translated into paper toys and paper dolls.

Animal paper dolls have been produced since before 1900. The earliest and perhaps most famous of these was a die-cut bear with five outfits and matching hats to be cut out. McLoughlin Brothers published *Tabby Cat* and *Jocco Monkey* in the 1880s. R. Tuck published both a cat and a dog, each with four outfits. R. Tuck was well known for its beautiful pantins or "mechanical marionettes" as they referred to them, which were operated by pulling a string, and for their "seesaws" which appeared just after the turn of the century. The Tuck Company also printed panoramas which folded out. These panoramas were sometimes of fairy tales like *Puss 'n Boots*; others were of the zoo, the circus and the farm. They came with animals and other characters that could be moved from slot to slot to create stories. Various boxed sets from the "Artistic Toy Novelty" series featured animals including "rockers," toys that rock back and forth, and the famous Tuck's "Noah's Ark Animals," a dozen pairs of animals that are cleverly joined together. These early toys were designed to teach as well as entertain, which the Victorians felt was important.

By 1907, America was in the midst of the Roosevelt Teddy Bear craze and the first Teddy Bear paper dolls were being manufactured. The earliest and perhaps most famous Teddy Bear was produced as a die-cut bear and five outfits with matching hats to be cut out. It was marketed in an envelope which has appeared printed with the labels of three different publishers — Selchow and Righter, Ottmann and E. I. Horsman.

The whole interest in the "Teddy Bear" was triggered, so the legend goes, by a hunting incident that occurred in November 1902. Roosevelt was on a hunting expedition in Mississippi. Hunting dogs chased a poor bear until it was too exhausted to fight. One of the men subdued the bear by hitting it on the head. When the President arrived, other members of the hunting party had already tied the animal to a tree. Feeling that it was unsportsmanlike, he refused to shoot the poor bear and asked that it be put out of its misery. *The Washington Post* printed the story on November 15. The next day cartoonist Clifford Berryman drew a political cartoon for the Sunday edition tying this incident to a political controversy between Louisiana and Mississippi. This was the first of a number of cartoons that he drew which included the "Teddy Bear." These cartoons prompted the birth of the cuddly creature that remains very popular today.

The Roosevelt bear was an instant success. The Ideal Company in America and the Steiff Company in Germany began producing stuffed "Teddy Bears." In 1909, *Pictorial Review* printed a wonderful bear based on the Roosevelt hunting incident entitled *Ted E. Bear Goes A-Hunting.*

At the end of his term of office, Roosevelt embarked on an extended hunting trip in East Africa, starting from Mombasa and including Nairobi, Lake Naivasha, Uganda and the Nile, and ending at Khartoum in December 1909. While on safari they hunted lion, hippopotamus, rhinoceros, leopard and elephant.

Following the interest in Roosevelt, the National Candy Company of Buffalo, New York, produced "The African Series" in 1910. The 16 pieces included a number of animals, African natives and several poses of Teddy Roosevelt as the hunter.

Soon after, many other companies were turning out furry figures. American Colortype produced a set of three cute animals, *Pretty Kitty, Dandy Doggie* and *Chubby Cubby.* These animals were printed in two sizes and sold boxed in several sets. The larger size was also sold individually in glassine envelopes.

Another set, *Doggy and Kitty Dolls*, was printed in Germany. It turns up much less often, but in some ways closely resembles the American Colortype set. It comes boxed with six separate sheets — three of dogs and three of cats. It is interesting to notice the similarities of some of the costumes, and even how similar *Dog B* is to *Dandy Doggie.*

The Gabriel Company produced a charming set of cats and dogs that were richly colored and heavily embossed. The animals have moving heads that cause their eyes to shift, much like some of their moving eye dolls.

Advertising has often used animal paper dolls to help promote products. Sometimes animals can more easily express the advertiser's message. Enameline Stove Polish produced a set of six animals, each dressed in amusingly appropriate costumes — the pig as a butcher, the fox as a pirate and the lamb as a maid. This set was probably available about the same time that the McLaughlin Coffee series of animals was being produced, but is less well known. The Behr-Manning Company of Troy, New York, produced *Barney Bear*, a paper doll to promote Barney's Sandpaper. They eventually printed four different sheets with *Barney Bear*. Fidelity Hams chose a plump pig to make their product more appealing. Bear Brand Hosiery created a walking paper doll to draw attention to their product.

Other animal paper dolls and paper toys appeared in the newspapers. Frequently, the newspapers ran paper toys for the children to cut out. These were mostly unsigned, and are usually hard to find because they were often thrown away. Some appear in color but many were simply black and white.

Magazines also picked up on the interest in animals with clothes. *The Woman's Magazine* published a delightful pair of rabbits in their December issue in 1919. They are interesting because not only do they have extra clothes, but their heads are designed to move. *Pictorial Review* also had a number of animals in their paper doll pages thanks to the artwork and imagination of Grace Drayton (see Chapter 8). *The Cottontail Family* drawn by Barbara Hale appeared in *McCall's Magazine* in April of 1920.

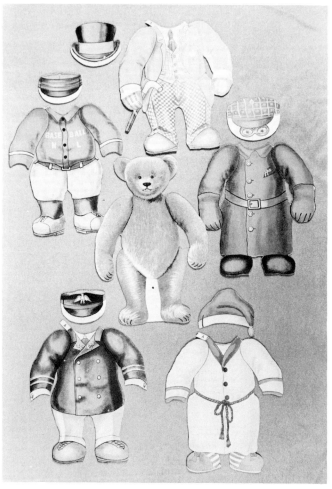

Illustration 284. 10½in (26.7cm) *Teddy Bear* with a wardrobe of five outfits and matching hats. The bear is die-cut but the clothing originally came in sheets to be cut out. The tabs on all of the costumes are marked "A." There is a baseball uniform with a red shirt, white pants and blue socks and a cap with a bill in blue with red stripes; a motoring coat in green and a red and green plaid cap with goggles; a yachting suit with a blue nautical jacket trimmed in gold, combined with white slacks and a blue cap with a red band and a gold eagle on the front; a yellow bathrobe trimmed with red lapels and red braid and belt and a night cap of red with a yellow band and a blue tassel; and a natty suit with a gray waist coat, red and buff tattersall vest, blue and white check trousers, cane and top hat.

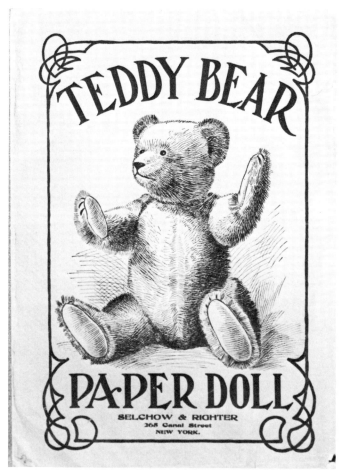

Illustration 285. Envelope for the *Teddy Bear*. It is marked "Selchow & Righter, 265 Canal Street, New York." This same envelope also appears marked, "J. Ottmann Litho. Co., N.Y." and "E. I. Horsmann, 365 Broadway, New York."

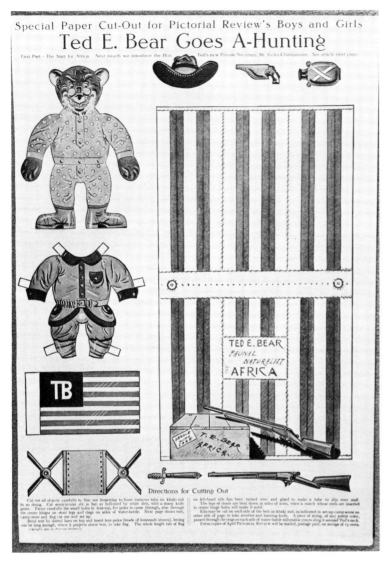

Special Paper Cut-Out for Pictorial Review's Boys and Girls

Ted E. Bear Goes A-Hunting

First Part – The Start for Africa.   Next month we introduce the Hon   Ted's new Private Secretary, Mr. Jocko Chimpanzee.   See article next page

TED E. BEAR
FAUNAL
NATURALIST
AFRICA

Directions for Cutting Out

Illustration 286. Ted E. Bear Goes A-Hunting appeared in *Pictorial Review*, April 1909. It was the first of a series of five paper doll pages. Each month a letter detailing Ted E. Bear's expedition through Central Africa accompanied the paper doll page. Other members of the expedition who appeared in the following months were: "Mr. Jocko Chimpanzee," personal secretary; "Rubber, the Fat Giraffe" guide; and "Goppo, the Elephant." The magazine also offered Ted E. Bear and the other animals printed on muslin with patterns for their wardrobes at 25 cents each.

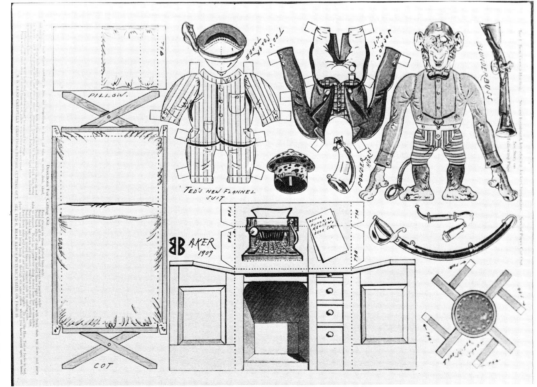

Illustration 287. Introducing Jocko Chimpanzee, second in the "Ted E. Bear" series, appeared in May 1909. It is signed by the illustrator, B. Baker.

Illustration 288. Teddy Roosevelt and his extended safari in Eastern Africa provided the idea for this unusual set. These pieces are from the "African Series" offered by the National Candy Company of Buffalo, New York. The complete set consists of 16 pieces and was printed in soft, natural colors by the P. R. Warren Company of Lowell, Massachusetts, copyright 1910. Pieces are: Elephant, Giraffe, Zebra, Hippopotamus, Marksman, Zebra and Hunter, Rhinoceros, Elephant Hunter and Dromedary.

BELOW: Illustration 289. These are the Africans from the "African Series" printed for the National Candy Company. The pieces are: African Cook, African Dude, Lion Hunter, African Pathfinder, African and African Belle.

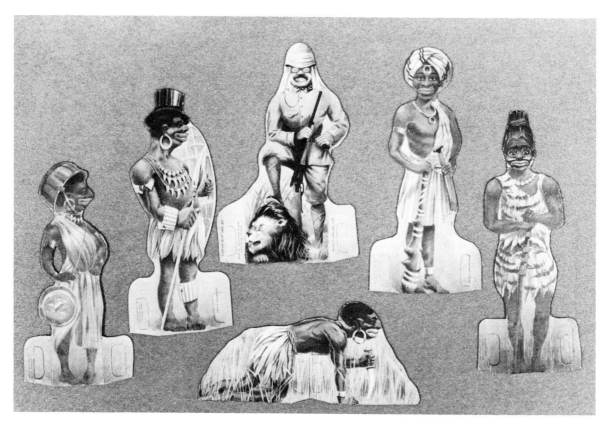

Illustration 290. 11in (27.9cm) *The Three Little Kittens* is one of the marionettes from "Father Tuck's Marionettes," a boxed set of ten figures that operate with a pull string. On the back of the marionette is a verse written by Clifton Bingham. The colors are beautiful and the marionette is deeply embossed, typical of so many of the Tuck toys. *McClelland Collection.*

Illustration 291. 11in (27.9cm) *Our Friends, the Bears* is also one of the marionettes from "Father Tuck's Marionettes." *McClelland Collection.*

Illustration 292. These brightly colored and embossed bears are one of the Tuck "Seesaws." *McClelland Collection.*

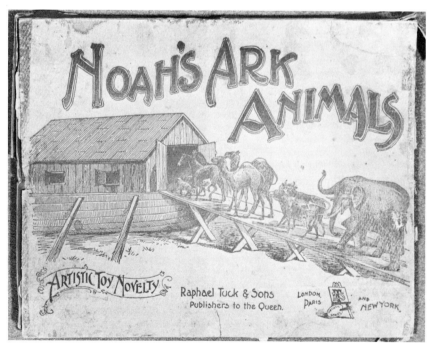

Illustration 293. Noah's Ark Animals from the "Artistic Toy Novelty" series was published by R. Tuck and Sons. It is a boxed set with 12 pairs of animals cleverly hooked together so that they can stand. *Edgar Collection.*

Illustration 294. Animals from "Noah's Ark Animals:" dogs, bears, deer and camels. *Edgar Collection.*

Illustration 295. Animals from "Noah's Ark Animals:" cats, goats, lions and horses. *Edgar Collection.*

Illustration 296. Animals from "Noah's Ark Animals:" tigers, donkeys, cattle and elephants. *Edgar Collection.*

AMERICAN COLORTYPE ANIMALS

The American Colortype Company produced three delightful animal pets, each with its own imaginative wardrobe. *Pretty Kitty*, *Dandy Doggie* and *Chubby Cubby* were printed in two different sizes, 5in (12.7cm) and 10in (25.4cm) and sold in sets and also separately. They were published boxed as a set in the small size as *Little Kitty Cut-Up and Her Playmates*. The three pets have also appeared in the larger size boxed as *Chubby Cubby Paper Doll Set* to cut and color by the American Crayon Company of Sandusky, Ohio.

Illustration 297. Little Kitty Cut-Up and Her Playmates is a boxed set including all three of the animals in the smaller size.

BELOW: Illustration 298. 5½in (14cm) *Pretty Kitty* comes with three outfits including a bridal gown, a deep blue coat trimmed with fur and a red blouse with a blue bow combined with a dark blue skirt and lots of accessories.

Illustration 299. 5¼in (13.4cm) *Dandy Doggie* comes with three outfits including tails and a top hat, a green Norfolk jacket with red lapels and cuffs combined with brown check pants and a red cap, and a blue military uniform with a silver eagle on the cap and accessories.

Illustration 300. 5in (12.7cm) *Chubby Cubby* comes with three outfits including an Indian costume with a full feather headdress, a pirate's outfit with a red shirt and purple pants and a blue sailor suit. Each outfit has appropriate extra accessories.

Illustration 301. Envelope for *Dandy Doggie.* Each of the larger size animals was sold separately in its own envelope. *McClelland Collection.*

159

DOGGIE AND KITTY DOLLS

This is an unusual boxed set which has six uncut sheets of animals printed on heavy paper. The colors are soft, beautiful and clear. Each sheet is marked "Germany," but there is no indication of the publisher. The set contains three dogs and three cats.

Illustration 302. Doggie and Kitty Dolls — box lid.

BELOW: Illustration 303. Uncut dog with two costumes, marked "B" on the tabs, from *Doggie and Kitty Dolls.*

Illustration 304. Uncut dog with two costumes, marked "C" on the tabs, from *Doggie and Kitty Dolls.*

Illustration 305. Uncut cat with two costumes, marked "D" on the tabs, from *Doggie and Kitty Dolls.*

Illustration 306. Uncut cat with two costumes, marked "E" on the tabs, from *Doggie and Kitty Dolls.*

Illustration 307. Uncut cat with two costumes, marked "F" on the tabs, from *Doggie and Kitty Dolls.*

*Note: the dog that is not shown is white. His costumes are a sailor suit and a red uniform with a drum. Each is marked "A" on its tabs.

Illustration 308. Each of these animals is marked with the Gabriel symbol on the back. They are deeply embossed and richly colored. Their heads move, causing them to roll their eyes. *McClelland Collection.*

Illustration 309. 5in (12.7cm) pig and 5½in (14cm) fox from the Enameline Stove Polish set of six animals. These sets were offered for three - two-cent stamps or two - two-cent stamps and three top labels from boxes of Enameline. *McClelland Collection.*

Illustration 310. Pig with his extra outfit as teacher is instructing everyone about "Fidelity" hams made by the Sinclair Company. *McClelland Collection.*

Illustration 311. Molly-Cottontail, and Pa and Buster Bunny appeared in *McCall's Magazine,* April 1920. The artwork was done by Barbara Hale who drew paper dolls regularly for the magazine. *McClelland Collection.*

Illustration 312. Miss Myrtle Duck appeared in the newspaper, but which one is uncertain. Someone has handwritten the date, August 7, 1932. *McClelland Collection.*

Illustration 313. This pair of rabbits appeared in *The Woman's Magazine* in December of 1919. The artwork was drawn by Bess Goe Willis. Notice how the heads slip into the bodies so that they can move their heads. (In 1920, *The Woman's Magazine* merged into *The Delineator*.) *McClelland Collection.*

BARNEY BEAR

A bear superimposed over an "M" was the symbol for the Behr-Manning Company, and *Barney Bear* was used by Behr-Manning, manufacturers of Barney's Sandpaper to advertise their sandpaper product. There were four different sheets of *Barney* printed by the company, which probably date from the 1930s.

Illustration 314. Barney Bear (the first sheet). *McClelland Collection.*

ABOVE RIGHT: Illustration 315. Barney Bear, Fourth Series. *McClelland Collection.*

RIGHT: Illustration 316. The Bear Brand Hosiery bear is a walking paper doll with feet that rotate as he moves along. *McClelland Collection.*

Two Talented Sisters — Drayton and Hays

Many people are familiar with famous Campbell Kids. Some know that they were originally created by the very talented Grace Drayton, but few know that she also had a very gifted sister, Margaret Hays. Together and individually, each had an outstanding career in the glamorous world of illustrating and publishing during the first quarter of the century.

These two talented sisters were born to George and Mary (Fitzgerald) Gebbie of Philadelphia, Pennsylvania. George Gebbie was an educated and successful art publisher and he believed in educating his daughters. Margaret was born first, July 31, 1874. She was tutored by her governess, later attending boarding school and the Convent of Notre Dame, Philadelphia. On October 14, 1877, when Margaret was three, Grace was born. The girls were undoubtedly exposed to drawing and painting at an early age. Most of Grace's education was also at private schools.

At the age of 19 Margaret married Frank Allison Hays. While the early years of her career are somewhat sketchy, Margaret became more involved with writing and Grace did more illustrating. By 1905, the sisters were publishing their combined work.

In 1900, at the age of 23 Grace married Theodore Wiedersiem. Grace's early work is often found signed "Wiedersiem." But this first marriage did not last and in 1911, she married for the second time. Her second husband was named W. Heywood Drayton III and it is only after 1911 that her work is found signed "Drayton."

In 1904, Grace began to design the Campbell Kids to advertise Campbell soup. The roly poly characters first appeared on trade cards, in magazine ads and on trolly cars. They were so popular that soon dolls were being produced. These dolls, with composition heads and stuffed bodies, were manufactured by the Horsman Company.

Both Margaret and Grace drew for *The Philadelphia Press*, but Grace's career took off more quickly and she soon added the *New York Journal, Associated Sunday Magazine, Sunday North American, The New York Herald, Scribner's Magazine, Cosmopolitan Magazine, The Ladies' Home Journal, Harper's Bazaar, The Delineator, Good Housekeeping, Pictorial Review* and *Saint Nicholas: An Illustrated Magazine for Young Folks*.

Margaret continued to illustrate but became much more noted for her writing. She designed paper doll books for M. A. Donohue and E. P. Dutton. She drew paper dolls for post cards, had many poems published in various magazines and wrote and drew for *Little Folks' Magazine* regularly.

Grace and Margaret collaborated on "Mother Goose Rhymes" which ran for five years in the *Associated Sunday Magazine*. "The Terrible Tales of Captain Kiddo" was one of their most famous endeavors. It appeared first in the *Sunday North American* and then was published in book form. Next followed a number of children's books all written by Margaret and illustrated by Grace.

Margaret Hays did continue to illustrate, however, and she produced the drawings for the *Mary Francis Cookbook*. She both illustrated and wrote for *Little Folks Magazine* regularly from 1912 to 1916. She also drew paper dolls which appeared in book form, such as "Fairy Favorite Cut-out Dolls" and "Fairytale and Flower Paper Dolls" for the M. A. Donohue Company.

When Grace began to work with *Pictorial Review Magazine* to produce her famous and always beloved Dolly Dingle series, Margaret was with her, providing wonderful verses to charm the children. These delightful pages entertained children for the next 20 years.

Grace, meanwhile, was designing prints, post cards, magazine covers, comic strips and dolls. Charles Scribner's Sons published many of her drawings as prints and they became so popular that post cards were soon created from them. The A. H. Davis Company of Boston, Massachusetts, and the Reinthal and Newman Publishers of New York also manufactured her post cards.

She designed a number of dolls but few of them have survived because so many were cloth and loved "to pieces." *Dolly Dollykins* and *Bobby Bobbykins* were designed in 1909. Made of cloth, these were probably her first dolls. *Kaptain Kiddo*, taken from the series she and her sister did for the *Sunday North American*, appeared in 1911. Louis Amberg and Sons patented *Dolly* and *Bobby* in 1910. With molded heads and stuffed bodies, these were her first composition type dolls. About the same time the Horsman Company introduced *Gee Gee Dolly* or *Peek-A-Boo* with its unbreakable head. Grace is also well known for her *Hug-Me-Tights* series of rag dolls which she designed around 1915. In 1923, the Averill Company registered *Chocolate Drop*, a brown rag doll that was very popular. The company soon followed with *Dolly Dingle* based on the *Pictorial Review* cut-outs.

In 1925, Margaret died but Grace carried on with her writing and illustrating. In 1931, the *New York American* began her comic strip, "Dolly Dimples and Baby Bounce" that ran for about a year. At the same time she drew another comic strip, "Kittens" that appeared on the same page with "Dolly Dimples and Baby Bounce" in some newspapers. Several years later she did "The Pussycat Princess" based on the character, Comfy, who had appeared in the earlier strip. She continued to work until her death in 1936.

THE SERIES IN PICTORIAL REVIEW

Dolly Dingle of Dingle Dell was first introduced in *Pictorial Review* in March, 1913, followed by *Billie Bumps* in April, *Kitty Cutie* in May and *Frisky Fido* in June. After these four sheets, Grace Drayton drew a series of theater pages and *Dolly Dingle* and her friends did not reappear until March of 1916. The following sheets are taken from the first continuous year of the series that ran almost without interruption until April of 1933 (*Dolly Dingle* did not appear during 1925 and from January until May of 1926). The characters drawn in these early pages are typical of Grace's style with their little "H" mouths, their wide eyes and their chubby bodies. Later in her career her style changed but she continued to return to many of the themes in these early pages for her inspiration.

Illustration 317. *Dolly Dingle of Dingle Dell,* **March** 1916.

Illustration 318. Billie Bumps of Dingle Dell, April 1916.

Illustration 319. Dolly Dingle as Queen of the May, May 1916.

Illustration 320. Dolly Dingle's Baby Brother, June 1916.

Illustration 321. Dolly Dingle's Little Sister Toodles, July 1916.

Illustration 322. Dolly Dingle on the Farm, August 1916. Varsolona Collection and Photograph.

Illustration 323. Sammy Snooks and His Pets, September 1916.

Illustration 324. Dolly Dingle's Halloween, October 1916.

Illustration 326. Dolly Dingle's Christmas Party, December 1916. (This is page one of a double page layout.)

Illustration 325. The Mousie Bride, November 1916.

Illustration 327. Dolly Dingle's Christmas Party — page two.

Illustration 328. Sammy Gets Ready for the Baseball Season, June 1920. This sheet shows one of the mask faces Grace designed for her paper dolls.

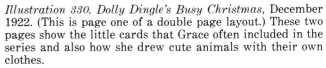

Illustration 330. Dolly Dingle's Busy Christmas, December 1922. (This is page one of a double page layout.) These two pages show the little cards that Grace often included in the series and also how she drew cute animals with their own clothes.

Illustration 329. Dolly Dingle Takes Up Light Opera — H. M. S. Pinafore, June 1921. During 1921, Grace drew a series of seven opera sheets that are popular with collectors today.

Illustration 331. Dolly Dingle's Busy Christmas — page two.

Illustration 332. Dolly Dingle's Kitty Dresses Up, April, 1923.
McClelland Collection.

Dolly Dingle's Little Friend Joey Goes to a Carnival

Drawings by GRACE G. DRAYTON

PARTY SLIPPERS

MASK CUT EYEHOLES OUT

TEDDY-BEAR HEAD CUT THE EYE-HOLES OUT

PARTY SUIT

HARLEQUIN SUIT FOR CARNIVAL

G.G.DRAYTON ©

JOEY

TEDDY-BEAR SUIT

JOEY'S LEGGINGS

JOEY'S HAT

JOEY'S OVER-COAT

DAY TIME DRESS.

Illustration 333. Dolly Dingle's Little Friend Joey Goes to a Carnival, January 1924. This sheet has been popular because it includes a Teddy Bear costume.

OTHER DOLLY DINGLE SHEETS

Dolly Dingle paper dolls occasionally appear printed on sheets of heavy cardboard. These were evidently licensed by *Pictorial Review* magazine. The Cincinnati Art Publishing Company published some of the sheets which came in paper envelopes marked "Dolly Dingle Cutouts for Kiddies." Laidlaw Brothers of Chicago, Illinois, advertised in 1928 that they offered four three-leaf folders containing "twelve series of cutouts; 120 pieces to cut out and play with; tied with handsome ribbon and packed in a glassine envelope with the lovliest Christmas book on which you write your Christmas greeting; a wonderful gift. All for $.50."

Illustration 334. Dolly Dingle and Sammy Go Skating. This sheet was printed by The Cincinnati Art Publishing Company and the same sheet appeared in *Pictorial Review* in January 1922.

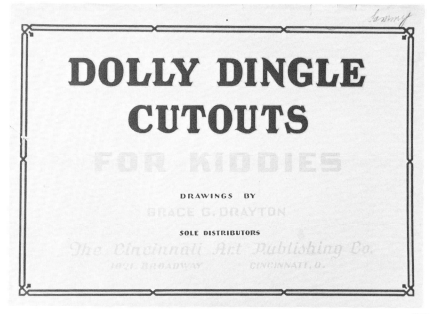

Illustration 335. Envelope for *Dolly Dingle and Sammy Go Skating.*

FAIRY FAVORITE CUT OUT DOLLS

Margaret Hays did the artwork for this paper doll book, "Fairy Favorite Cut Out Dolls" (No. 671), which was printed by M. A. Donohue and Co. of Chicago, Illinois, copyright 1913.

Illustration 336. "Fairy Favorite Cut Out Dolls" (No. 671) — cover.

Illustration 337. Red Riding Hood, "Fairy Favorite Cut Out Dolls."

Illustration 338. Cinderella, "Fairy Favorite Cut Out Dolls."

BO-PEEP

Illustration 339. Bo-Peep, "Fairy Favorite Cut Out Dolls."

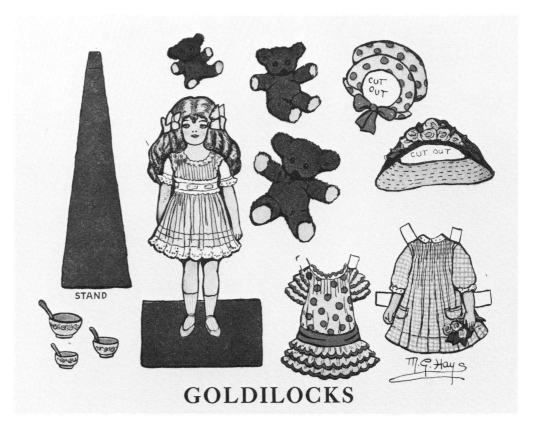

Illustration 340. Goldilocks, "Fairy Favorite Cut Out Dolls." (Fatima and Sleeping Beauty pages are not shown.)

GOLDILOCKS

NURSERY FAVORITE CUT-OUT DOLLS

Margaret Hays did the artwork for this paper doll book, "Nursery Favorite Cut-Out Dolls" (No. 672), which was printed by M. A. Donohue and Co. of Chicago, Illinois, copyright 1913. The two books were later combined into "Fairy-Tale and Flower Paper-Dolls," No. 675.

Illustration 341. "Nursery Favorite Cut-Out Dolls" (No. 672) — cover.

Illustration 342. Poppy, "Nursery Favorite Cut-Out Dolls."

Illustration 343. Forget-Me-Not, "Nursery Favorite Cut-Out Dolls."

FORGET-ME-NOT

LILY OF THE VALLEY

Illustration 344. Lily of the Valley, "Nursery Favorite Cut-Out Dolls."

Illustration 345. Pansy, "Nursery Favorite Cut-Out Dolls."

PANSY

181

Illustration 346. Daisy, "Nursery Favorite Cut-Out Dolls."

Illustration 347. Rose, "Nursery Favorite Cut-Out Dolls."

POST CARDS

Margaret Hays illustrated a number of paper doll post cards. The "Doll Series" is especially interesting. There are eight different post cards, each with the names of two dolls but only one doll appears on each card. The clothing is designed to fit not only the doll on the card but also a companion doll on another card. These post cards are numbered. The series includes: No. 1 - *Lottie and Dottie*, No. 2 - *Dottie and Lottie*, No. 3 - *Letty and Betty*, No. 4 - *Betty and Letty*, No. 5 - *Molly and Polly*, No. 6 - *Polly and Molly*, No. 7 - *Billy and Bobby*, No. 8 - *Bobby and Billy*. The post cards give no clue about who published them.

Illustration 348. Dottie and Lottie, "Doll Series No. 2."

Illustration 349. Betty and Letty, "Doll Series No. 4." Fertel Collection.

LITTLE FOLKS' ANNUAL 1913

Little Folks' Magazine was published by the S. E. Cassino Company for a number of years. Margaret Hays was a steady contributor to the publication with her poems and drawings. In 1912, she began a series of paper dolls about Polly Patten, a little American girl, and her trip abroad. The first paper doll, *Polly Patten*, herself, appeared in October 1912. With each paper doll came a letter from *Polly* telling about her experiences in the various countries that she visited. These letters were all written by Margaret Hays. This series continued through December of 1913. Each year the monthly magazines were offered in an annual hardbound volume. The following paper dolls appeared in the *1913 Little Folks' Illustrated Annual*. (*Polly*, herself, does not appear in this Annual, nor does *Zara of Delhi* who appeared in the December issue of the magazine.)

Marie of Paris

Gretchen of Munich

Kathleen of Queenstown

ABOVE: Illustration 350. Gretchen of Munich. (Also appeared in *Little Folks' Magazine*, December 1912.)

ABOVE RIGHT: Illustration 351. Marie of Paris. (Also appeared in *Little Folks' Magazine*, January 1913.)

RIGHT: Illustration 352. Kathleen of Queenstown. (Also appeared in *Little Folks' Magazine*, November 1912.)

Valentina of Rome.

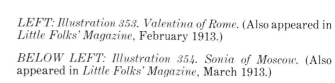

LEFT: *Illustration 353. Valentina of Rome.* (Also appeared in *Little Folks' Magazine*, February 1913.)

BELOW LEFT: *Illustration 354. Sonia of Moscow.* (Also appeared in *Little Folks' Magazine*, March 1913.)

BELOW: *Illustration 355. Mary Cavendish.* (Also appeared in *Little Folks' Magazine*, April 1913.)

Sonia of Moscow.

Mary Cavendish.

Donald MacGregor
(See page 238)

LEFT: *Illustration 356. Donald MacGregor.* (Also appeared in *Little Folks' Magazine*, May 1913.)

BELOW LEFT: *Illustration 357. Delores and Pedro.* (Also appeared in *Little Folks' Magazine*, June 1913.)

BELOW: *Illustration 358. Katinka.* (Also appeared in *Little Folks' Magazine*, August 1913.)

Delores and Pedro.

Katinka.

186

Illustration 359. Yo San. (Also appeared in *Little Folks' Magazine*, October 1913.)

LITTLE FOLKS' ANNUAL
1915

The following paper dolls created by Margaret Hays appeared in the *1915 Little Folks' Annual* and also in the monthly magazines of the same year.

Illustration 360. Little Boy. (Also appeared in *Little Folk's Magazine*, August 1915.) *Ferguson Collection and photograph.*

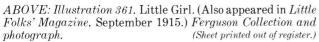

ABOVE: Illustration 361. Little Girl. (Also appeared in *Little Folks' Magazine,* September 1915.) *Ferguson Collection and photograph.*   *(Sheet printed out of register.)*

ABOVE RIGHT: Illustration 362. Baby. (Also appeared in *Little Folks' Magazine,* October, 1915.) *Ferguson Collection and photograph.*   *(Sheet printed out of register.)*

Illustration 363. Lady. (Also appeared in *Little Folks' Magazine,* November 1915.) *Ferguson Collection and photograph.*

Betty Blue and her Mammy Daphne

Illustration 364. Betty Blue and Her Mammy Daphne. (also appeared in Little Folks' Magazine, December 1915.) Ferguson Collection and Photograph.

Illustration 365. Little Red Riding Hood with Some Now-A-Days Frocks. (Also appeared in Little Folks' Magazine, January 1916). Ferguson Collection and photograph.

Little Red Riding Hood with some now-a-days frocks.

CANADIAN HOME JOURNAL SHEETS

Grace Drayton drew a series of paper dolls which appeared in the *Canadian Home Journal*. They were reproduced in black and white with one color added. They are interesting because of the touches she added to make her characters seem more typically Canadian.

Illustration 366. Kathleen and Her Kitty, October 1928.

Illustration 367. The Christmas Skating Girl, December 1928. (Notice similarity to Dolly Dingle and Sammy Go Skating.)

Illustration 368. The Skating Partner, February 1929. (Notice similarity to *Dolly Dingle and Sammy Go Skating*.)

Illustration 369. Just a School Day Reminder, March 1929.

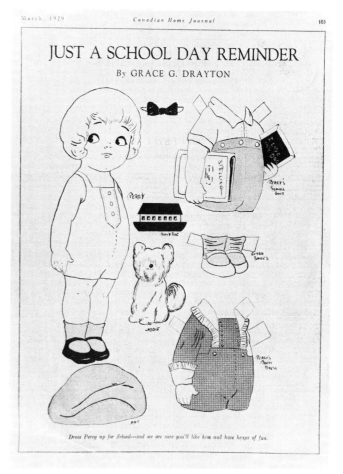

Chapter 9

Kewpies Forever

Among the fairies, sprites and little poeple are the ever-joyous Kewpies. These wonderful cherubs are the inspiration of one Rose O'Neill. Rose was born in Wilkes-Barre, Pennsylvania, June 24, 1874. Her parents were Alice Asenath and William Patrick O'Neill. She was their second child. She had an older brother, John Hugh, and after her, Mary Ilena, James and Callista were born. Her father was a publisher and a bookseller who also collected books. He and his wife spent much time reading literature to their children. After Rose was born the family moved to Nebraska where they lived from 1883 to 1889. Rose's early education was from the Convent of the Sacred Heart in Omaha. It was here that Rose won an art contest for the best drawing by a Nebraska school child. The contest was sponsored by the *Omaha World-Herald* newspaper and she received a five dollar gold piece for her prize. This contest discovered the artist that was to become the highest paid illustrator of the times.

Rose gained fame as a poet, a novelist, and most of all as an illustrator, a talent which she taught to herself. Her father wanted her to become an actress and at the age of 15 she went to New York to finish her education. She lived at the Convent of the Sisters of St. Regis. She paid for three years of her studies by selling drawings to magazines. She met Playboy Gray Latham and married him when she was only 18. But after only five years he died.

Her early work was published in *Life, Harper's, Good Housekeeping, Collier's, Cosmopolitan, Puck* and *Truth*. At *Puck* she not only illustrated but wrote short stories and verses, and soon joined the staff. There she met and eventually married the editor of *Puck*, Harry Leon Wilson.

Their relationship lasted for some years during which she illustrated two of his books. They traveled to Europe where she gained more insight into the arts. After her return in 1908, however, she and her husband separated and she returned to Missouri where her parents were then living. Bonniebrook, the O'Neill home in the Ozark Mountains, became her refuge. It is here that she had many of her inspirations, and many believe that the Kewpies were born here after her separation from Wilson.

She said that the Kewpies came to her in a dream in her childhood, and that she was inspired by her brother as a baby and all of her early memories of babies. The tiny top-knot was from the little curl on top of his head and the wings were because babies are half angel. She said that the name "Kewpie" was baby talk for "Cupid" because it looked funnier spelled "Kew."

These frolicing Kewpies are ever-present to teach, to help, to comfort, but most of all to bring joy and love. The Kewpies give aid to the fairies, teach bad little boys to change their ways, and rescue unfortunate animals in danger. The first Kewpies appeared in illustrated verses on the pages of *The Ladies' Home Journal* in 1909. *The Woman's Home Companion* introduced the Kewpie Kutouts in 1912. They were also eventually published in the *The Delineator* and *Good Housekeeping*. Rose created a home for them in "Kewpieville," a land of constant merriment where each holiday is celebrated gaily and no problem is too great to be solved. In 1925, she added Scootles, the traveling Kewpie who was "always scooting off to find trouble."

Quickly the Kewpies were produced as dolls. The first ones were made in Germany for the George Borgfeldt Company. They were made of bisque and came in many sizes. The Kewpies became very popular with adults and Rose designed a series of figurines which are referred to as "Action Kewpies." Over 30 different factories were turning out bisque Kewpies at one time. Joseph Kallus, a well-known doll artist, worked with Rose to design the *Kewpie* dolls for the Borgfeldt Company. In the twenties, Kallus founded the Cameo Doll Company and began manufacturing his own line of *Kewpie* dolls in the United States, first in composition and later in vinyl.

Because of her great success with the Kewpies, people are not always familiar with her work as an artist and as a sculptor. Rose O'Neill was a member of the Societe des Beaux Arts and exhibited some of her artwork at the Paris Salon. She drew some mystical figures which she called "Monster Drawings" or "Sweet Monsters." These are very different from her Kewpies. They are huge, groping, twisted and somehow sad. She said they symbolized the union of the divine and the animal. In April of 1921 she had a one-woman exhibit of these "Sweet Monsters" in the Galerie Devambez in Paris which greatly surprised the art world.

In her writing and her artwork at this time she showed an interest in legend and myth. She wrote several novels, *Garda* in 1929 and *The Goblin Woman* in 1930. She struggled with intellect, tragedy and morality combined with legend and myth. This work was criticized and never really accepted very well by the art community.

Rose also had great success in illustrating advertisements. She did the artwork for many Jell-O ads and for special Jell-O advertising booklets. To advertise Hendler's Ice Cream she drew full color pictures of Kewpies eating ice cream for advertising cards. Kellogg's, Lifebuoy Soap, Colgate's Cashmere Bouquet Soap and Talc Powder, Eastman Kodak and Oxydol Soap all commissioned her for various magazine ads but none ran any series of her drawings regularly.

She had a colorful social life because she liked to surround herself with talented people. At her Washington Square apartment in New York City she entertained constantly and her friends included Kahlil Gibran, the Booth Tarkingtons and Birger and Matta Lie. Her group of friends were known as "The Court" and she was "The Queen." She loved having friends around. Some people who came stayed only a few days, others for a year or more.

She also enjoyed traveling and spent much time in Europe. She brought back many art treasures with her. When her mother became ill she moved to Bonniebrook where she lived with her sister until her death in 1944. She left the world her philosophy and her ever-joyous and loving Kewpies.

THE KEWPIE KUTOUTS

The "Kewpie Kutouts" were the first paper dolls of the Kewpies drawn by Rose O'Neill. They appeared in *Woman's Home Companion* almost monthly from 1912 to 1914. With each of the Kewpie Kutout pages she also wrote an accompanying page of illustrated verse about the Kewpies' adventures. The following series is complete.

Illustration 371. "The First of the Kewpie Kutouts," *Presenting Wag, the Kewpie Chief; Dotty Darling, and Dotty Darling's Baby Brother,* October 1912.

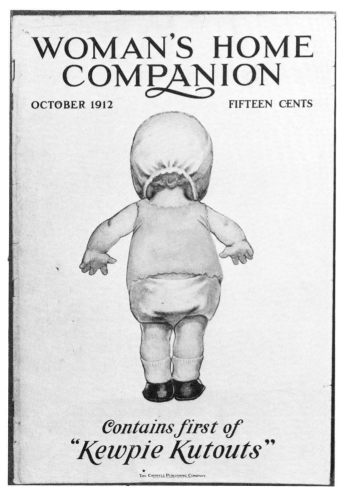

Illustration 370. Rose O'Neill drew the cover for the October 1912 issue of the *Woman's Home Companion* magazine introducing the "Kewpie Kutouts."

193

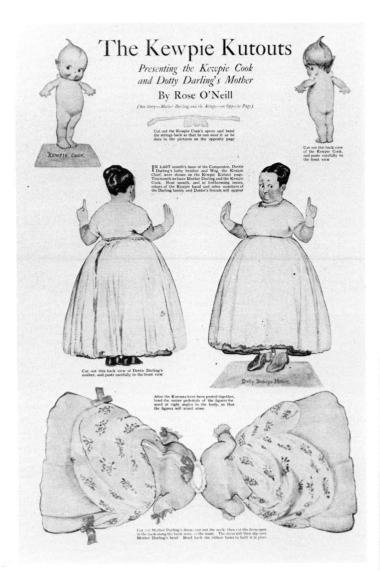

Illustration 372. "The Kewpie Kutouts," *Presenting the Kewpie Cook and Dotty Darling's Mother*, November 1912.

Illustration 373. *Stern Irene and the Kewpie Gardener*, "Third in the Series of Kewpie Kutouts," December, 1912.

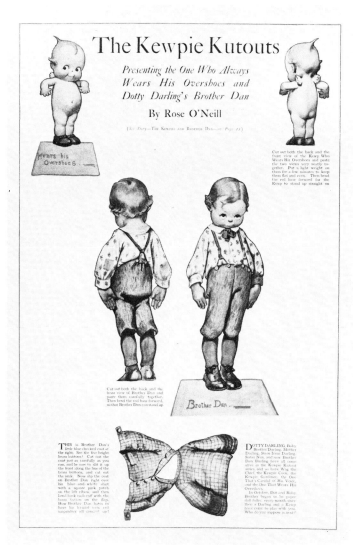

Illustration 375. "The Kewpie Kutouts," *Presenting the One Who Always Wears His Overshoes and Dotty Darling's Brother Dan*, February 1913.

Illustration 374. "The Kewpie Kutouts," *Presenting the One that's Careful of his Voice and Dotty Darling's Sister Nan,* January 1913.

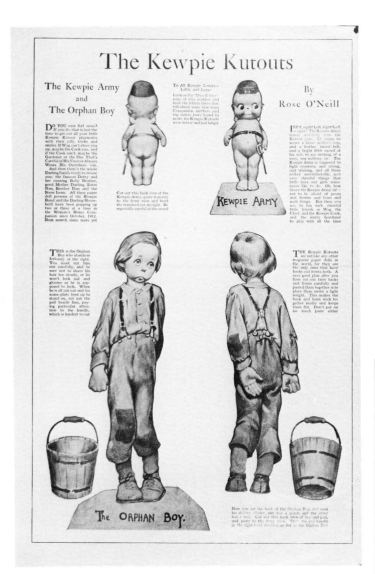

Illustration 376. "The Kewpie Kutouts," *The Kewpie Army and The Orphan Boy,* March 1913.

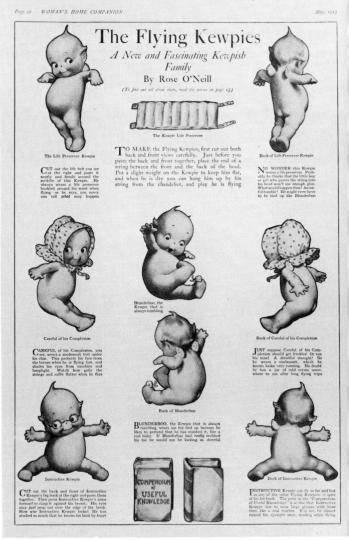

Illustration 377. "The Flying Kewpies," *A New and Fascinating Kewpish Family,* May 1913.

Illustration 379. *Dotty and Four of Her Kewpie Friends*, July 1913.

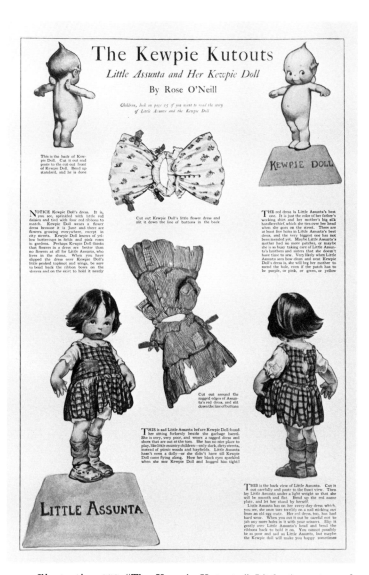

Illustration 378. "The Kewpie Kutouts," *Little Assunta and Her Kewpie Doll*, June 1913.

Illustration 380. The Musical Kewpies and the Little German Girl, August 1913.

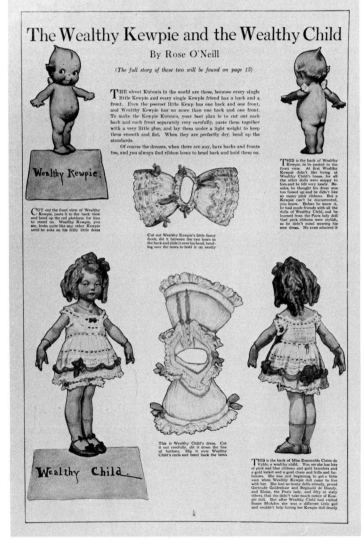

Illustration 381. The Wealthy Kewpie and the Wealthy Child, September 1913.

Illustration 383. The Kewpie Dog and the Bad Little Boy, December 1913.

Illustration 382. The Kewpie Nurse and the Better Baby, October 1913.

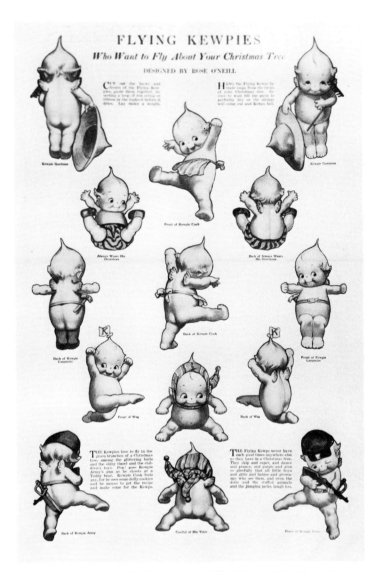

Illustration 384. Flying Kewpies Who Want to Fly About Your Christmas Tree, January 1914.

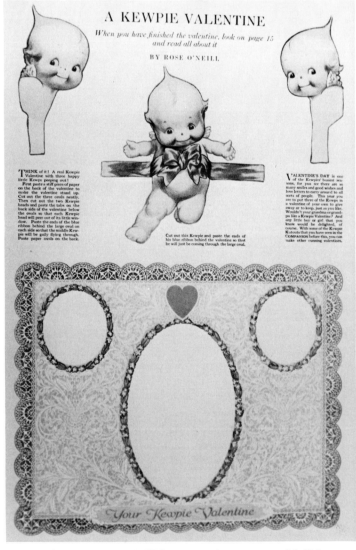

Illustration 385. A Kewpie Valentine, February 1914. McClelland Collection.

KEWPIES WITH RAGSY AND RITZY CUT-OUT DOLLS
- W969

Rose O'Neill's "Kewpies with Ragsy and Ritzy Cut-Out Dolls" was published by Whitman Publishers, copyright Rose O'Neill 1932. Ritzy had previously appeared in the Kutout pages as the "Wealthy Child," who was becoming too vain, and Ragsy as "Little Assunta," who was very, very poor and did not even have a doll.

Within this paper doll book is a little book to cut out and assemble with the story of Ragsy and Ritzy.

As the story goes Ragsy Brown was a poor little girl and Ritzy's parents were rich. Ritzy was a little too proud of her looks, her family's wealth and her pretty clothes. Ritzy did not like Ragsy's clothes. So the Kewpies decided to teach Ritzy a lesson. They dressed her in Ragsy's clothes and Ragsy in hers, and then Ritzy saw that Ragsy was "a perfect Dear." Ritzy was never proud again. The Kewpies gave Ragsy a Hugsome Kewpie and the girls became best friends.

Illustration 386. Cover.

Illustration 387. Inside cover.

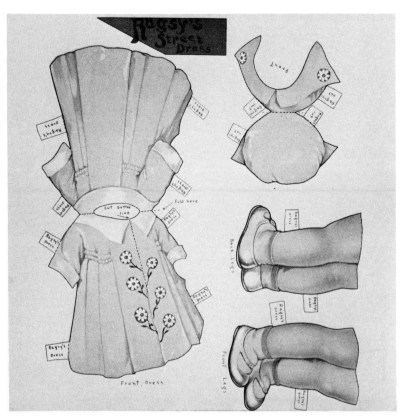

Illustration 388. Page 1.

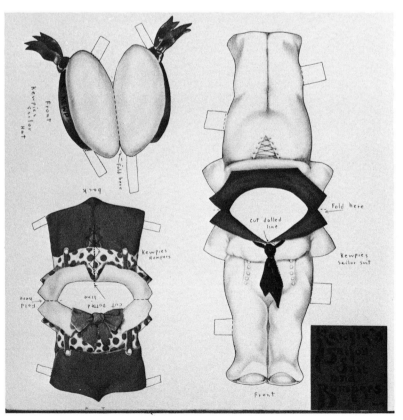

Illustration 389. Page 2.

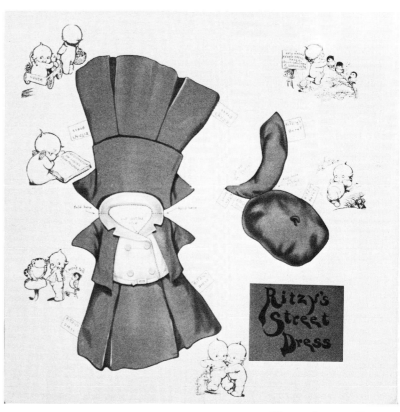

Illustration 390. Page 3.

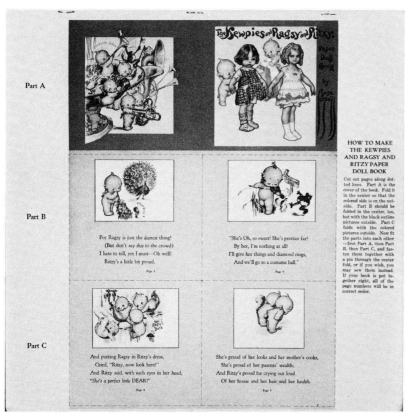

Part A

Part B

Part C

HOW TO MAKE THE KEWPIES AND RAGSY AND RITZY PAPER DOLL BOOK

Cut out pages along dotted lines. Part A is the cover of the book. Fold it in the center so that the colored side is on the outside. Part B should be folded in the center, too, but with the black outline pictures outside. Part C folds with the colored pictures outside. Now fit the parts into each other—first Part A, then Part B, then Part C, and fasten them together with a pin through the center fold, or if you wish, you may sew them instead. If your book is put together right, all of the page numbers will be in correct order.

Illustration 391. Page 4.

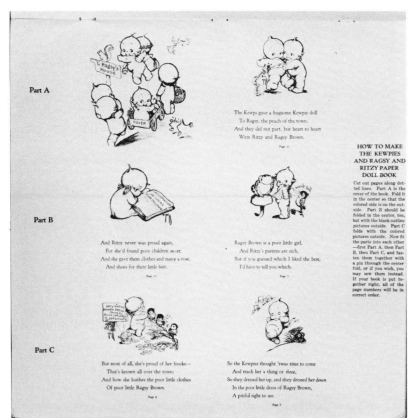

Part A

Part B

Part C

The Kewps gave a hugsome Kewpie doll
To Ragsy, the peach of the town,
And they did not part, but heart to heart
Were Ritzy and Ragsy Brown.

Page 11

And Ritzy never was proud again,
For she'd found poor children sweet,
And she gave them clothes and many a rose,
And shoes for their little feet.

Page 10

Ragsy Brown is a poor little girl,
And Ritzy's parents are rich,
But if you guessed which I liked the best,
I'd have to tell you which.

Page 3

But most of all, she's proud of her frocks—
That's known all over the town;
And how she loathes the poor little clothes
Of poor little Ragsy Brown.

Page 4

So the Kewpies thought 'twas time to come
And teach her a thing or three,
So they dressed her up, and they dressed her down
In the poor little dress of Ragsy Brown,
A pitiful sight to see.

Page 7

HOW TO MAKE THE KEWPIES AND RAGSY AND RITZY PAPER DOLL BOOK

Cut out pages along dotted lines. Part A is the cover of the book. Fold it in the center so that the colored side is on the outside. Part B should be folded in the center, too, but with the black outline pictures outside. Part C folds with the colored pictures outside. Now fit the parts into each other—first Part A, then Part B, then Part C, and fasten them together with a pin through the center fold, or if you wish, you may sew them instead. If your book is put together right, all of the page numbers will be in correct order.

Illustration 392. Back of page 4.

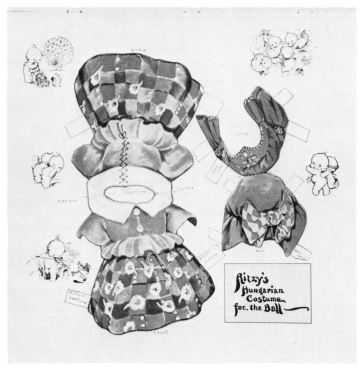

Illustration 393. Page 5.

Illustration 394. Page 6.

Illustration 395. Inside back cover.

Illustration 396. Back cover.

SCOOTLES AND KEWPIE DOLL BOOK - S2131

"Scootles and Kewpie Doll Book" was published by the Saalfield Publishing Company, copyright 1936 Rose O'Neill. Scootles got her name because she was always scooting off on tours. She was the first tourist to get to Kewpieville.

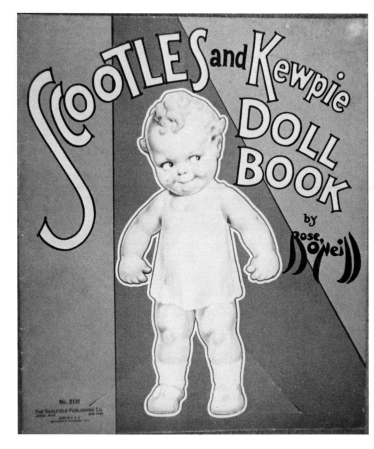

Illustration 397. Front cover. *McClelland Collection.*

BELOW: Illustration 398. Inside front cover. *McClelland Collection.*

BELOW RIGHT: Illustration 399. Page 1. *McClelland Collection.*

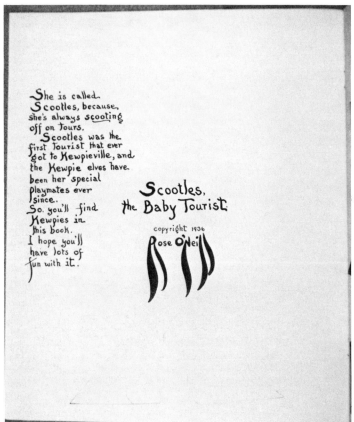

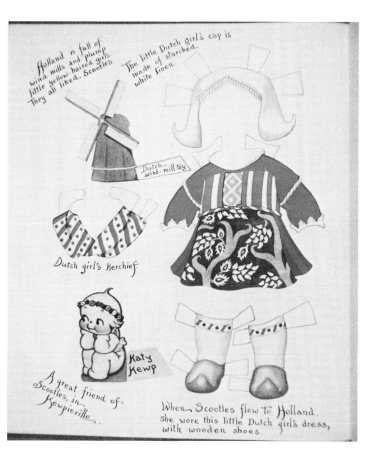

Holland is full of wind-mills and plump little yellow-haired girls. They all liked Scootles.

The little Dutch girl's cap is made of starched white linen.

Dutch wind-mill toy.

Dutch girl's Kerchief.

Katy Kewp

A great friend of Scootles, in Kewpieville.

When Scootles flew to Holland she wore this little Dutch girl's dress, with wooden shoes.

Scootles' little bird dress.

You can slip her Jap. doll under this hand.

Scootles' Japanese house-robe.

Her duck play dress and hat.

Johnny Kewp and Katy Kewp

Let's not cut out between the heads.

Her Japanese doll.

Illustration 400. Page 2. McClelland Collection.

ABOVE RIGHT: Illustration 401. Page 3. McClelland Collection.

RIGHT: Illustration 402. Page 4. McClelland Collection.

Slip Scootles' face in front of tab.

One of Scootles' favorite summer costumes.

Scootles bought this dress from a little girl in Poland.

This little dress is very becoming to the little tourist.

ABOVE LEFT: *Illustration 403.* Page 5. *McClelland Collection.*

ABOVE: *Illustration 404.* Page 6. *McClelland Collection.*

Illustration 405. Page 7. *McClelland Collection.*

ABOVE: Illustration 406.
Page 8. McClelland Collection.

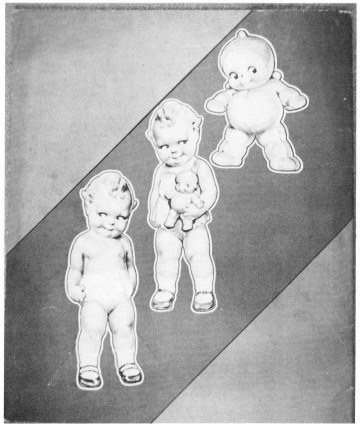

Illustration 407. Back cover.
McClelland Collection.

Brownies, Delightful Brownies

The Brownies are irresistible little imps who love to frolic in the twilight hours while the rest of the world sleeps. They have an immense curiosity and a continuing quest for fun. They are enthusiastic, never lazy. They offer kind service and good deeds to those in need. They do good for the sake of good and not for any reward. Brownies have magical powers. Sometimes their experiences end in disaster but they always escape unharmed. Their many adventures have taken them ice skating, tobogganing, bicycling, ballooning and canoeing. They try all the things that little girls and boys enjoy. They have explored the circus, gone to school, played baseball and sailed the seas.

These delightful, fun-loving characters were the inspiration of illustrator Palmer Cox. They first appeared in *Saint Nicholas: An Illustrated Magazine for Young Folks* in the 1880s. Cox was a Canadian, born in Granby, Quebec, on April 28, 1840. His parents, Michael and Sarah, were immigrants to Granby, a Scottish settlement which was near the United States border of Vermont. His father was Irish and his mother Scottish. The many legends that Cox grew up with from his rich Scottish and Irish heritage undoubtedly provided the inspiration for the wonderful little imps he created. He graduated from the Granby Academy at the age of 17 and left to visit the eastern part of the United States. He drifted west and by the age of 23 he had settled in San Francisco, California. Cox worked first as an employee of the railroad and then in the nearby shipyards. In his spare time he wrote for local newspapers. It was in San Francisco that he began to study sketching. Success did not come to him quickly. The western newspapers did not offer much financial encouragement to a struggling illustrator. In 1875, at the age of 35, his first book, *Squibb's of California* or *Everyday Life Illustrated* was published. Soon after he was offered a job with a comic newspaper, *Wild Oats*, and moved to New York where there was more opportunity for him. There he opened a studio, and began to work regularly for *Saint Nicholas: An Illustrated Magazine for Young Folks*, *Merriman's Weekly*, *Little Folks'*, *Harper's Young People* and *Wide Awake*. He became well known for his humorous sketches accompanied by rhymes. Many of his comic drawings of animals were used for advertisements.

The Brownies, which he began to draw in the 1880s, gave him something distinctive and throughout the rest of his career, he continued to develop and expand their adventures. At first the Brownies acted only as a band but as time progressed, certain characters began to emerge. He continued to add little characters until there were over 40 from all over the world. The Dude became his most popular sprite.

The Brownies' Ride, his first book of the Brownie series, was published in 1883. Over the years he produced 13 books about the Brownies. All but one of these books were written in verse. More than one million copies of these volumes were sold before his death. It has been said by *The New York Times*, "It is doubtful whether any fashion in children's literature has ever swept a country so completely as Palmer Cox's Brownies took possession of the American childhood in the early eighties."

Palmer Cox eventually returned to Granby and built "Brownie Castle" where he spent his summers. He died on July 24, 1924, at "Brownie Castle," leaving a wonderful heritage to children's literature.

The Brownies were so popular with the children that they were soon translated into paper toys to delight the little ones. Companies had the Brownies printed to advertise their products. Lion Coffee produced two extensive series of Brownies and packed one set in each pound of coffee. One series featured the "Standing Brownies." Twenty-five different characters have been identified. Each Brownie is two pieces, body and head. All are interchangeable, creating hundreds of comic combinations. The other series, "Riding Brownies" also feature two pieces. This time it is a Brownie and an animal. The little sprites are cleverly combined with some political overtones such as Uncle Sam riding a buffalo.

The New York Biscuit Company also produced a similar set of Brownies, under the license of Palmer Cox. These sprites were in two pieces, but not as easily interchangeable because their heads slipped up between the front and back of their bodies and were held in place by their hands. This series was made up of 16 different characters.

Cordova Coffee Company manufactured Brownies which were to be collected and each had a different letter on his chest. The idea was to spell "Cordova Coffee" and win a premium.

The Bee Soap Brownies were fashioned very much like the Lion Coffee ones with a head that slipped easily onto the body.

LION COFFEE STANDING BROWNIES

The Lion Coffee Company, a subsidiary of the Woolson Spice Company, offered a set of Brownies which have come to be called the "Standing Brownies." To promote their coffee they packaged one Brownie in each pound of their coffee. The Brownies came in two pieces — a head and a body. Each piece was marked with the character's name on the head tab and on the base, but the pieces were interchangeable and children could create hundreds of comic combinations. To date 25 different Brownies have been identified. These Brownies were patented and copyrighted 1892 by Palmer Cox, and licensed by the Arnold Print Works. The various characters were taken directly from Cox's verses. They were printed by the Thomas & Wylie Litho. Company of New York.

Illustration 408. Sage, Dutchman and Canadian.

Illustration 409. Policeman, Scotchman and Russian.

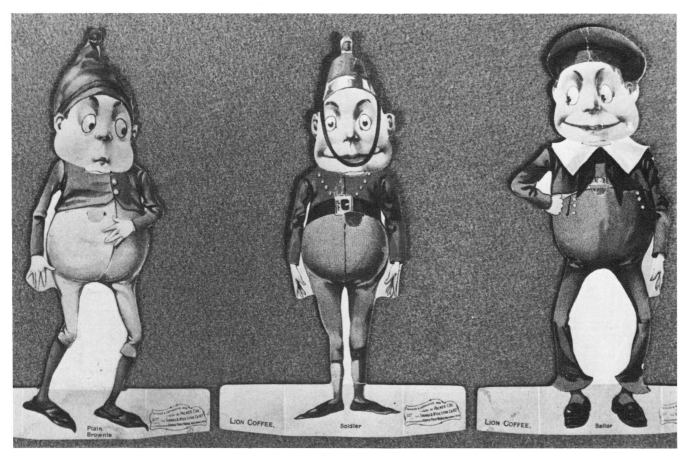

Illustration 410. Plain Brownie, Soldier and Sailor.

Illustration 411. Japanese, Uncle Sam and Indian.

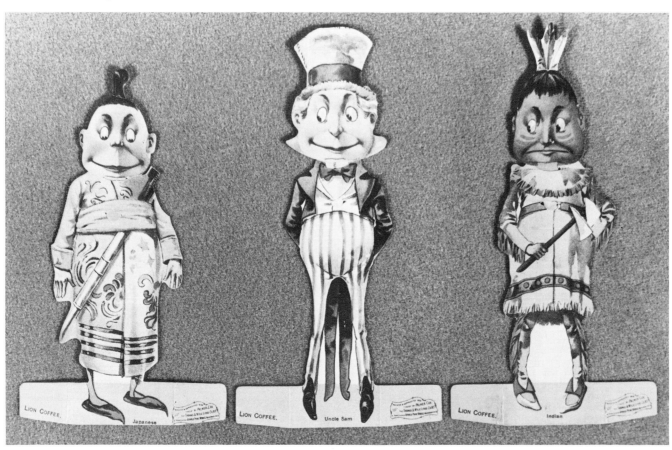

Illustration 412. King, Englishman and *Dunce.*

Illustration 413. Frenchman, Dude and *Esquimau.*

Illustration 414. German Peasant, Chinaman and *East Indian.*

Illustration 415. Turk, Irishman and *Student.*

** Missing: *Jockey* — No complete list of these Brownies has been found. These are the Brownies currently identified. There may be others.

LION COFFEE RIDING BROWNIES

The Lion Coffee Company also created a second set of Brownies. This set has been named the "Riding Brownies" because each of the characters in the series is riding an animal. Again, there are two pieces. This time it is a Brownie and an animal. These Brownies were also packaged in the coffee. Political satire was often present in the choice of animal each Brownie is riding. Again, the combinations created by interchanging the Brownies and their animals are often quite comical. On the base of each of the animals appears the name of that animal and the Brownie that originally came with it which is helpful for identification.

Illustration 416. *King* on lion, *Student* on zebra and *Spaniard* on bull.

Illustration 417. Uncle Sam on bison, *Canadian* on moose and *Jockey* on horse.

215

Illustration 418. Scotchman on doe, *Esquimau* on polar bear and *Sage* on giraffe.

Illustration 419. Dude on donkey, *Indian* on panther and *Turk* on camel.

Illustration 420. Dutchman on black bear, *Policeman* on rhinoceros and *East Indian* on elephant.

216

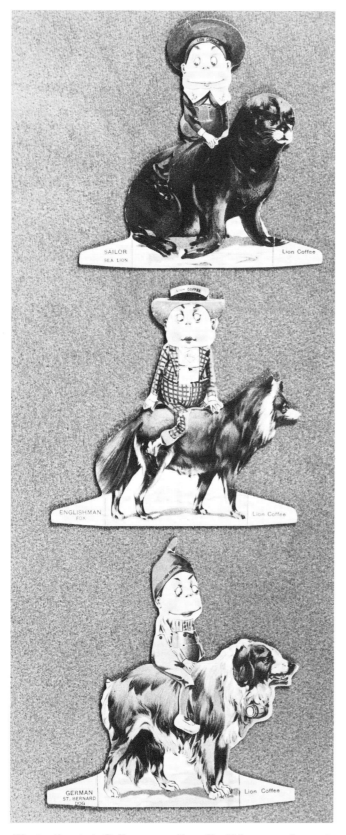

Illustration 422. Chinaman on tiger, *Soldier* on kangaroo and *French* on chamois.

Illustration 421. Sailor on sea lion, *Englishman* on fox and *German* on St. Bernard dog.

LEFT: Illustration 423. Russian on wolf, *Irishman* on pig and zebu (Japanese is not shown).

** Missing: *Italian* on sheep — No complete list of these Brownies has been found. These are the Brownies with animals known to date. There may be others.

BELOW: Illustration 424. These 5¼in (13.4cm) Brownies, which look very much like the Lion Coffee Brownies, were offered by the New York Biscuit Company. The set of 16 were available in exchange for four - two-cent stamps. The Brownies were printed by the Gast Company of New York, copyright 1894. They were not licensed by Palmer Cox. Shown in the picture from left to right are: *The Chinaman, The Spaniard, The Turk,* (top) *English Officer, The Scotchman, The Dude* and *The Irishman. Edgar and Musser Collections.*

RIGHT: Illustration 425. This 7in (17.8cm) Brownie has been cut out. He is printed front and back and is unmarked. The costume in the upper left has a nautical motif. The jacket is blue with a white collar and the pants and shirt are also white. The hat is white with red and blue trim. In the upper center is a yellow stocking cap with red and green stripes. The beard is white. The jacket below is red trimmed with gold buttons and a brown belt with a gold buckle. The oriental costume in the upper right is yellow with a red and green flowered print. The hat is a silver blue and matches the pants under the kimono. In the lower left is an Irish costume with a green jacket, gold pants and a red shirt accompanied by a gray hat with a green band. The Brownie, himself, is dressed in a brown jacket with tan and brown striped pants. In the lower right is a blue police officer's coat trimmed with gold buttons and a gold belt and a gray helmet with a gold insignia marked "N.Y."

BELOW: Illustration 426. These 5in (12.7cm) Brownies were offered by the Cordova Coffee Company. Each Brownie has a black letter printed on the front. The same letter does not always appear on the same Brownie. By saving the letters to spell "Cordova Coffee" and sending a two-cent stamp for postage, the company would send a free gold ring. The Brownies were printed by the George S. Harris & Sons, Lith., N.Y. Left to right: *The Dutchman, The Soldier* and *The Chinaman.*

ABOVE: Illustration 427. This sheet of Brownies appeared as a Sunday Art Supplement to *The Boston Sunday Globe,* December 8, 1895. When cut out, the pieces from this page fit into slots on a theater stage which the newspaper offered.

LEFT: Illustration 428. This Brownie was offered to advertise Bee Soap. The heads of the Bee Soap Brownies were interchangeable like the Lion Coffee Brownies. This series was also licensed by the Arnold Print Works under the Palmer Cox copyright. *McClelland Collection.*

Celebrated Royalty

The lives of Royalty hold a great fascination for many people. It is always interesting to follow the lives of those who shape nations. Through the centuries monarchs caused wars and prevented them; they managed the nations' economy and ruled over their subjects. Royalty led a life of endless routine before the public, with many ceremonies and appearances requiring their royal presence. These people had every advantage given to them and led glamorous and colorful lives which people of lesser means love to dream about. This exclusive class of royal figures represents the ruling families of Europe, and the world.

During the 19th century the controlling families of Europe had intermarried and were all closely related. There were four great families remaining in Europe at this time, the Saxe-Coburg Windsor (of Great Britain), the Romanov (of Russia), Hapsburg (of Austria-Hungary) and Hohenzollern (of Germany). With Queen Victoria the reigning monarch in Great Britain, her children married into the other major monarchies of the continent. Her oldest daughter, Victoria, was married to the Crown Prince of Prussia and mother of Wilhelm II. Her son, Edward, heir to the British throne, married Princess Alexandra of Denmark. Alexandra's sister eventually became Queen of Russia as wife to Alexander III. Victoria's youngest daughter, Beatrice, was mother to Victoria Eugenie, wife of Alfonso III, the King of Spain. Victoria's granddaughter, Alix, married Nicholas II of Russia.

During this period many paper dolls were being made of members of royal families. Many of the paper dolls of these royal figures were made in Germany and were of the German royalty. *Kaiserin und Prinzesschen* is a wonderful boxed set with die-cut pieces produced in rich color and embossed. The Kaiserin is Auguste Viktoria, wife of Kaiser Wilhelm II of Prussia, with her daughter, Viktoria Luise. Auguste Viktoria was a popular figure and appeared often in the early German paper dolls. Kaiser Wilhelm II was the subject of several sets with his various uniforms. Also popular were Kromprinz Wilhelm, the heir apparent, and Eitel Friedrich, his oldest brother, as well as the other children in the royal family, seven in all. Irene of Hesse, wife of Kaiser Wilhelm's brother, Heinrich, has also been immortalized in paper dolls.

Paper dolls of Royalty are usually easy to recognize because their clothing is so lavish. These figures are often shown in their state and ceremonial garments which are far richer than anything worn by their subjects. Identifying them is not always as easy, but many pictures exist and from them clues can sometimes be found.

The Queens and Martha Washington Paper Dolls was published by the Stokes Company and was designed to be instructional as well as entertaining to the children. This set selects the most outstanding queens from history and shows them with their court robes and reception costumes.

Queen Isabella of Spain (1451-1504) was Queen of Castile. She married Ferdinand V of Aragon, uniting Spain's two largest kingdoms. Together they drove the Moors out of southern Spain and made it a Christian kingdom. Queen Isabella also supported Christopher Columbus, giving Spain large holdings in the western hemisphere.

Queen Elizabeth I of England (1533-1603) was another of the queens included. Called "Good Queen Bess," she was the daughter of Henry VIII and Ann Boleyn. During her reign England experienced great commercial prosperity and a great colonial empire began. Although she was vain and had a bad temper, she was known as a master of diplomacy. During her reign she reestablished The Church of England as the official religion of the country.

Queen Marie Antoinette of France (1755-1793), whose reign ended in tragedy, was controversial if not always popular. She was beautiful, gay and extravagant. The daughter of Emperor Francis I and Maria Theresa of Austria, she married the crown prince of France at the age of 15 and lived at Versailles. There she grew bored and was not in touch with the realities of the times. She and Louis XVI died in the guillotine during the French Revolution.

Martha Washington (1732-1802) was included as the First Lady of the United States. She was the daughter of a wealthy Virginia planter. After the death of her first husband, she became one of the wealthiest women in Virginia. She was a woman of great charm and ability. She met and married George Washington and when he became President, she presided as his hostess with grace and dignity.

Queen Louise of Prussia (1776-1810) married

Frederick Wilhelm II and became queen in 1797. She was very popular with her people for her grace, beauty, generosity and, in time of war, courage. She was queen during the time that Napoleon was attacking Prussia.

Queen Victoria of England (1819-1901) ruled wisely and capably for 63 years. When she came to the throne the monarchy was not respected, but over the years the English people grew to love and admire her. During her reign England flourished with industrial development and the country reached its greatest power with colonial expansion all over the world.

Queen Margherita of Italy was Italy's first queen. Born in Savoy, she became the wife of King Umberto I, son of Vittorio Emanuele II, who ascended the throne in 1878. Margherita loved the arts and music. Tragedy came when King Umberto I was assassinated in 1900. Her son became Vittorio Emanuele III.

The McLaughlin Coffee Company chose some of the same great ladies of their similar series. They chose Queen Isabella, Queen Marie Antoinette, Queen Marguerite of Italy, Queen Elizabeth and Martha Washington. But they also included Mary, Queen of Scots, the Czarina of Russia and the Crown Princess of Sweden.

Mary, Queen of Scots (1542-1587), the daughter of James V of Scotland, became the Queen of Scotland when she was a week old. She was educated in France and married the Crown Prince of France. He died soon after becoming king, and she returned to Scotland where she reigned as queen, and then married Henry Stuart. After her husband's death she was forced to abdicate and she eventually fled to England to seek help from her cousin, Queen Elizabeth, who saw her as a rival to the throne of England and had her imprisoned. Nineteen years later she was accused of a plot to kill Elizabeth and, while she declared her innocence, she was found guilty and beheaded.

The Czarina of Russia was the Princess Dagmar of Denmark, sister of Queen Alexandra, wife of Edward VII, King of England. She was married to Alexander III and took the name, Marie Feodorovna, after her marriage. The Czarina was only 22 when she was coronated. She loved the lavish court life in St. Petersburg after growing up with limited means in Denmark. She bore five children. After her husband's death she continued to appear in public as the Dowager Empress with her son, Nicholas II.

The Crown Princess of Sweden was Victoria, wife of Prince Gustaf, later Gustaf V. The Swedish royal family was very popular with the people. Prince Gustaf's father ruled Norway and Sweden and tried to keep them united, but one year before his death and Gustaf's ascension to the throne the two countries separated.

McLoughlin Brothers created several paper dolls of royal figures. *Madame Pompadour*, one of the most intriguing ladies in history, appeared in one of the penny folders McLoughlin Brothers advertised in the 1880s. These inexpensive paper dolls were designed to be available for those on even a modest income and were always of very appealing characters.

Madame Pompadour was a lady with a sort of "Cinderella" story. She was born a member of the middle class in France and yet became paramour to the King and lived lavishly at Versailles for the rest of her life. As a young woman she married the nephew of a wealthy financier, Lenormand d'Etoiles, who through his uncle introduced her to French high society. Louis XV was quite taken with her and she became his mistress. She provided him with entertainment and gay living and continued to have great influence over him in politics after their affair had ended. King Louis gave her the title "Marquise de Antoinette Poisson" and an estate of her own but she chose to remain at Versailles.

The Marquis and *The Marchioness* were also printed by McLoughlin Brothers. They are regal in every way with titles and fine wardrobes, but they do not resemble any specific royal figures. With them children's imagination could explore the exclusive world of the rich and powerful.

Some companies chose royalty for advertising their products. Czar Baking Powder does not mention Czar Nicholas II but the picture looks very much like him. The Shaker Salt Company advertised that their salt appeared on royal tables all over the earth and published a folder of paper dolls of royal figures.

Royalty, ever before the public eye, continues to fascinate and entertain us. These historical figures provide a wonderful way for collectors to learn more about famous events through the personal experiences of those who shaped them.

LEFT: *Illustration 429. Kaiserin und Prinzesschen — box lid. McClelland Collection.*

BELOW: *Illustration 430.* 6½in (16.5cm) *Kaiserin* and 3in (7.6cm) *Prinzesschen* from *Kaiserin und Prinzesschen,* are representations of Kaiserin Augusta Victoria, wife of Kaiser Wilhelm II of Prussia, and their daughter, Viktoria Luise. This rare and wonderful boxed set has rich color and is deeply embossed. The costumes for these dolls include their court robes, reception gowns and lavish garments for occasions of state. There is also an ornate jewel box containing the Kaiserin's jewels. *McClelland Collection.*

E. S. TUCKER FAMOUS QUEENS AND MARTHA WASHINGTON

Famous Queens and Martha Washington Paper Dolls was a very special boxed set of paper dolls printed in full color on a series of sheets of high quality paper to be cut out. Elizabeth S. Tucker did the water-color sketches for this set in soft tones, which was published by the Frederick A. Stokes Company, copyright 1895. The set was designed to be educational as well as entertaining. The historical characters and their costumes including their "robes of state" and "reception gowns" were carefully drawn to be accurate. The Stokes Company was a publisher of deluxe children's books.

RIGHT: *Illustration 431.* Queen Isabella of Spain, 1492, was important in uniting Spain and restoring Christianity. The doll has blue eyes and black hair. She is wearing a white dress. Her other costumes include in the upper right: crown of state and court robe; lower left: walking costume with headdress and coronet; lower right: reception robe.

BELOW: *Illustration 432.* Famous Queens and Martha Washington Paper Dolls — cover.

Illustration 433. Queen Elizabeth of England, 1558, was the daughter of Henry VIII and Ann Boleyn. During her reign England had great commercial prosperity and began a far-reaching colonial empire. The doll has brown hair and eyes and is wearing white petticoats covered by a white robe trimmed with yellow ribbons. Her other costumes include in the upper left: court robe; lower left: walking costume and bonnet; lower right: reception robe.

Illustration 434. Queen Marie Antoinette of France, 1789, was the beautiful wife of Louis XVI, whose reign as Queen of France ended in tragedy when she and Louis were beheaded by their subjects. This doll has brown eyes and wears a white powdered wig. Her gown is white. Her other costumes include in the upper right: court robe; lower left: reception robe; lower right: Trianon garden costume. Each of her costumes has a matching headdress.

Illustration 435. Martha Washington, 1775, a woman of great charm and ability, was the wife of the first President of the United States. A gracious hostess, *Martha* has brown eyes and her white hair is covered with a cap. She is wearing a printed pink top over a white skirt. Her other costumes include in upper right: walking costume and bonnet; lower left: reception gown and head dress; lower right: costume of state with headdress and shawl combined.

Illustration 436. Queen Louise of Prussia, 1797, wife of Frederick Wilhelm II, was very popular with her subjects and very brave when Napoleon was attacking Prussia. The doll has brown hair and blue eyes. She is wearing a blue print empire gown trimmed with matching blue ribbons. Her other costumes include on the upper left: court robe; lower left: walking costume with bonnet or headdress; lower right: reception gown.

226

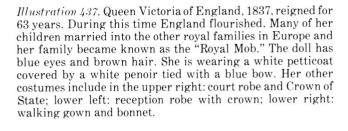

Illustration 437. Queen Victoria of England, 1837, reigned for 63 years. During this time England flourished. Many of her children married into the other royal families in Europe and her family became known as the "Royal Mob." The doll has blue eyes and brown hair. She is wearing a white petticoat covered by a white penoir tied with a blue bow. Her other costumes include in the upper right: court robe and Crown of State; lower left: reception robe with crown; lower right: walking gown and bonnet.

Illustration 438. Queen Margherita of Italy, 1868, was Italy's first queen. She loved the arts and music. Tragedy came when her husband, King Umberto I, was assassinated. The doll has blonde hair and blue eyes. She is wearing a blue robe lined in pink over her white petticoat. Her other costumes include in the upper right: reception robe; lower left: court robe and headdress; lower right: walking costume and bonnet.

Illustration 440. Queen Victoria of England Paper Dolls — cover page. McClelland Collection.

QUEEN VICTORIA
OF ENGLAND
(1837)

PAPER DOLLS

With Court Robe and Crown of State; Reception Robe with
Crown; and Walking Gown

BY

ELIZABETH S. TUCKER

Artist of "A Year of Paper Dolls," etc.

NEW YORK
Copyright, 1895, by
FREDERICK A. STOKES COMPANY
PUBLISHERS

Mc LAUGHLIN COFFEE COMPANY QUEENS

The McLaughlin Coffee Company advertised a series of paper dolls of famous queens to help promote their coffee. One set was packaged in each pound of their coffee. There were eight different queens in the series, and each set consisted of four pieces including a doll, costume pieces and a piece of furniture. Information about the furniture is on the back of each doll. All of the pieces are marked "McLaughlin's XXXX Coffee, Patent Applied For." The series was printed by the J. Ottmann Lith. Co. of N.Y.

ABOVE: Illustration 441. Queen Elizabeth with her court robe, crown and dresser.

RIGHT: Illustration 442. Queen Isabella with her court costume, crown. (Rocker not shown.)

Illustration 443. Marie Antoinette with her extra costume (in two pieces) and sideboard. Midwest Paper Doll Quarterly.

Illustration 444. Crown Princess of Sweden and her folk costume and cabinet.

Illustration 445. Czarina of Russia with her reception costume and screen. Midwest Paper Doll Quarterly.

Illustration 446. Mary Queen of Scots with her extra costume and a standing mirror.

Illustration 447. Martha Washington with her extra costume and bookcase.

Illustration 448. Queen Marguerite of Italy with her ceremonial robes and table. *Midwest Paper Doll Quarterly.*

McLOUGHLIN BROTHERS ROYALTY

In the 1880s, the McLoughlin's Brothers printed several paper dolls using royalty as their theme. They printed a penny folder of *Madame Pompadour* and for a dime, the more deluxe sets of *The Marquis* and *The Marchioness*, a realistic pair based on 18th century nobility. They were quick to offer paper dolls of several celebrities of the time like Tom Thumb and his troup but they did not produce any paper dolls of contemporary royal figures.

BELOW: Illustration 449. 4in (10.2cm) *Madame Pompadour* from the "Mulligan Guard Series" was printed, front only, in a penny folder to be cut out. One of the most intriguing ladies in history, she was mistress to Louis XV, King of France. She led a gay and exciting life at the Palace of Versailles.

RIGHT: Illustration 450. The Marquis — folder.

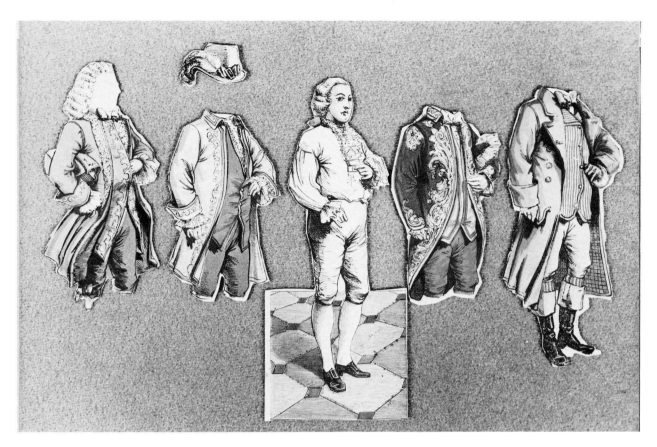

ABOVE: Illustration 451. 5in (12.7cm) The Marquis, Series No. 2, was originally printed in booklet form to be cut out. His four costumes are all printed front and back. (One of his hats is not shown.) While he is not known to be a portrait of a royal figure, he gives every representation of his exclusive class. (A "Marquis" is a French nobleman with rank above a "Duke" or an "Earl.")

BELOW: Illustration 452. 5⅜in (13.6cm) The Marchioness, Series No. 2, is a companion set to The Marquis. These sets originally sold for ten cents in the 1880s. This paper doll with her four costumes and one known hat (which is not shown) was printed front and back in booklet form to be cut out. Like the Marquis, this royal figure is not known to be a portrait of a historical figure.

GERMAN ROYALTY

During the last quarter of the 19th century German Royalty was a favorite topic for many of the paper dolls printed in Germany where printing was done so well. Generally, these paper dolls have fine detail, beautiful color and are often deeply embossed. Some of the paper dolls came die-cut and elegantly boxed, but many more of these paper dolls originally appeared in large sheets to be cut out. Sometimes there were a number of sheets in a single set. It is interesting to notice that these paper dolls' clothes usually do not have tabs but a drop of wax was used to hold the clothing in place. The costumes often have a discoloration where the wax was placed. Today, almost all information about these printing companies and the wonderful paper dolls that they produced has been lost because of time and the ravages of two wars.

LEFT: *Illustration 453.* This 7¾in (19.8cm) nobleman advertised for Czar Baking Powder. He bears a great resemblance to Czar Nicholas II, the reigning Czar during the 1890s and into the 20th century but his name is not specifically mentioned. *McClelland Collection.*

BELOW: *Illustration 454.* 6⅜in (16.1cm) *Augusta Victoria,* wife of Kaiser Wilhelm II.

ABOVE: *Illustration 455.* 6½in (16.5cm) *Irene of Hesse*, wife of Heinrich, brother of Kaiser Wilhelm II.

ABOVE RIGHT: *Illustration 456.* 6¾in (17.2cm) *Kaiser Wilhelm II. McClelland Collection.*

RIGHT: *Illustration 457.* 4⅝in (11.8cm) *Kromprinz Friedrick Wilhelm*, oldest son of Kaiser Wilhelm II and heir to the Prussian empire.

Illustration 458. 4⅛in (10.5cm) *Prinz Eitel Fredrick,* second son of Kaiser Wilhelm II and second in line to inherit the Prussian empire.

Illustration 459. 6¾in (17.2cm) unidentified lady. *McClelland Collection.*

Index

Paper Dolls are listed in the Index alphabetically by their first names.

A

A&P Tea Company, 73, 118
Adele, The Delineator, 130
Advertising, 151-152, 193
  A&P Tea Company, 73, 118
  Ayres Patent Medicine, 3, 10
  Bear Brand Hosiery, 152, 166
  Bee Soap Company, 211, 220
  Behr-Manning Company, 152, 166
  Clark's ONT Spool Cotton, 3, 11, 113
  Cordova Coffee Company, 210, 219
  Czar Baking Powder, 222, 234
  Dinsmore dresses, 86, 109-110, 127-128
  Domestic Sewing Machine Company, 59
  Economy Pattern Company, 3, 9
  Enameline Stove Polish, 152, 163
  Excella Fashion Book, 86, 107, 118
  Fidelity Hams, 152, 164
  Hood, C.I., Company, 16-17, 51-52, 114
  Lion Coffee, 210, 211-218
  McLaughlin Coffee Company, 3, 9, 152, 222, 229-231
  Miles, Dr., Medical Company, 70-71, 116
  Minard's Company, 86, 94-95
  Munsingwear Company, 86, 108, 130, 140
  National Candy Company, 120, 151, 154
  Nestle Company, 72
  New York Biscuit Company, 210, 218
  Pope Manufacturing Co., 16, 26-28
  Prima Donna Corsets, 30
  Singer Sewing Machine Company, 3, 9
  Woolson Spice Company, 211
"African Series, The," National Candy Co. 120, 151, 154
Albert, Prince, 15, 16
Alice, Woolworth Co., 91
"American Beauties," 68-69
American Colortype Company, 64, 85, 96, 128-129, 151, 158-159
  Chubby Cubby, 121, 151, 158-159
  Dandy Doggie, 121, 151, 158-159
  Little Kitty Cut-Up and Her Playmates, 158-159
  Patriotic Dressing Dolls, 128-129
  Pretty Kitty, 121, 151, 158
American Three-Color Company, 64, 128
American Lady, McLoughlin Bros., 15, 20
Amlico Company
  Our Favorite Dolls, 64, 67
American Lithograph Company, 64, 67
"Artistic Toy Novelty" series, R. Tuck, 151, 156
A.T. Company, 64
Ayres Patent Medicine, 3, 10
Alexandra, Queen, 3, 74, 221
Art Nouveau, 74
Auguste Viktoria, Kaiserin, 221, 234

B

Baltimore American, The, 130
Barney Bear, 152, 166
Bear Brand Hosiery, 152, 166
Beatrice, Woolworth Co., 91-92
Bee Soap Brownies, 211, 220
Behr-Manning Company, 152, 166
Berryman, Clifford, 151
Betsy Brunette, McLoughlin Bros., 15, 23
Betty, Minard's, 94
Betty and Lettie, 183
Betty Bonnet, Ladies' Home Journal, 3, 130
Betty Is Going Away To Boarding School, Gabriel Co., 100
bloomers, 16
Bingham, Clifton, 155
Bobby, The Boston Sunday Globe, 128
Bobby and Betty, the Excella Twins, 86, 107, 118
"Boston Herald Ladies," 16, 30-50
Boston Post, The, 130
Boston Sunday Herald, The, 16, 30
Boston Sunday Globe, 128, 230
"Bridal Party Series of Dressing Dolls," R. Tuck, 3, 6-8, 112
Bride, The, McLoughlin Bros., 2, 4
Bride No. 0102, McLoughlin Bros., 12
Bride and Her Trousseau, The, R. Tuck, 3, 6, 112
Bridegroom, R. Tuck, 3, 7, 112

Bridegroom and Groomsman, McLoughlin Bros., 2, 5
Bridesmaid, McLoughlin Bros., 2
Bridesmaid, The, R. Tuck, 3, 6, 8, 112
Brooklyn Times, The, 30
Brownies, 123, 210-220
Buffalo Sunday News, 74, 75
bustle, 2, 15-16, 54
Butterick, 75
"Butterick Family," 144-145
Butterick patterns, 84

C

Campbell Kids, 167
Canadian Home Journal, 190-191
Chester, Carolyn, 84, 130, 141-143
Chicago Record, The, 30, 33, 43, 44
Chubby Cubby, American Colortype Co., 121, 151, 158-159
Cincinnati Art Publishing Company, The, 177
Cincinnati Commercial Gazette, 30, 34
Clara, Clark Austin & Smith, 15, 18-19
Clara West, McLoughlin Bros., 19, 18-19
Clark, Austin & Smith, 15, 18-19, 53
  Clara, 15, 18-19
Clark's ONT Spool Cotton, 3, 11, 113
  Dolls' Wedding Series, 3, 11, 113
  Wedding Set, 11
Columbia bicycles, 16, 26-28
Cordova Coffee Company, 210, 219
Cottontail Family, The, McCall's, 152, 164
Cox, Palmer, 210-211
crinoline, 2
Crocker, W.M., 82
cycling, 8, 16, 26-28, 29, 36
Czar Baking Powder, 222, 234

D

Dagmar of Denmark, Princess, 3, 222, 230
Daisy and her Dresses, J. W. Spear Co., 88
Dandy Doggie, American Colortype Co., 121, 151, 158-159
Darling Daisy and Her Dresses and Hats, Gabriel Co., 98
"Darling, The" Series of New Dressing Dolls, Gabriel Co., 98
Dean and Son Limited, 54
Dear Dorothy, R. Tuck, 60
Delineator, The, 4, 14, 75, 84, 106, 130, 141, 144, 165, 192
Designer, The, 106
Diane, the Bride, McLoughlin Bros., 3, 5
Dinsmore Dresses, 86, 109-110, 127-128
Dinsmore, Elsie, 86
Die Schwestern, 17, 111
Doggie and Kitty Dolls, American Colortype Co., 151, 160-162
Doll Bride, Ayres Co., 3, 10
"Doll Series" postcards, 183
  Betty and Lettie, 183
  Dottie and Lottie, 183
"Dolls For All Seasons," R. Tuck, 60-61
Dolls' Wedding Series, Clark's ONT, 3, 11, 113
Dolly Darling, Gabriel Co., 86, 97
Dolly Dear, Gabriel Co., 86, 96
Dolly Delight, Gabriel Co., 86, 97
Dolly Dingle, Pictorial Review, 130, 167-177
"Dolly Dingle Cutouts for Kiddies," 177
"Dolly Sheets," Gabriel Co., 102-103
"Dolly Varden" series, McLoughlin Bros., 15, 23
Domestic Sewing Machine Company, 59
Donohue, M.A., and Company, 85, 167, 178-181
  "Fairy Favorite Cut Out Dolls," 178-179
  "Nursery Favorite Cut-Out Dolls," 180-181
  "Fairy-Tale and Flower Paper Dolls," 180
Dottie and Lottie, 123, 183
Drayton, Grace, 121, 167-177, 190-191
Dutton, E. P., 167

E

Economy Pattern Company, 3, 9
Edith, Dr. Miles, 71, 116
Edward VII, King, 74
Eitel Friedrich, 221, 236
Elizabeth I of England, Queen, 126, 221, 222, 225, 229
Elsie Dinsmore, 86, 109-110, 127-128

Enameline Stove Polish, 152, 163
embossed paper dolls, 5, 16, 25, 53, 57, 86, 113, 117, 119
  Auguste Victoria, 234
  Die Schwestern, 17, 111
  Irene of Hesse, 125, 221, 235
  Kaiserin und Prinzesschen, 124, 221, 223
  Kaiser Wilhelm II, 125, 235
  Kromprinz Friedrick Wilhelm, 221, 235
  Lady Cyclists Up To Date, 16, 29
  Our Little Treasure, 3, 13, 112
  Prinz Eitel Friedrich, 236
Eugenie de Montijo, 2
Ever-New Doll, The, Gabriel Co., 99
Excella Fashion Book, 86, 107, 118

F

"Fairy Favorite Cut Out Dolls," M. A. Donohue and Company, 178-179
"Fairy-Tale and Flower Paper Dolls," M. A. Donohue and Company, 180
Famous Queens and Martha Washington Paper Dolls, Stokes Publishing Company, 126, 221, 224-228
Fanny Fairleigh, R. Tuck, 74, 81
Farm and Home Magazine, 128
Farquharson, 86
Father Tuck's Doll Sheets, 6
Father Tuck's Marionettes, 155
Fidelity Hams, 152, 164
Findley, Martha, 86
Fisher, Harrison Cady, 74
Flossie, Selchow and Righter, 63
Fluffy Ruffles, Ottmann Litho., 74, 80
Frank Leslie's Magazine, 16
Friedrick Wilhelm, Kromprinz, 221, 235

G

Gabriel, Samuel, and Sons Company, 85-86, 96-106, 130, 150, 163
  Betty Is Going Away To Boarding School, 100
  Darling Daisy and Her Dresses and Hats, Gabriel Co., 98
  "Darling, The" Series of New Dressing Dolls, Gabriel Co., 98
  Dolly Darling, 86, 97
  Dolly Dear, 86, 96
  Dolly Delight, 86, 97
  "Dolly Sheets," 102-103
  Ever-New Doll, The, 99
  "My Book of Darling Dolls," 104-106
  Susan, 101
  Winkle Family, The, 130, 150
Gibson, Charles Dana, 74
Gibson Girl, 2, 74
Gibson Girl of the Sunday News, 75-79
Godey's Lady's Book, 16
Grace, Dr. Miles, 70
Grandmother's Tea Party, A&P Tea Company, 73, 118
Good Housekeeping, 4, 167, 192
Graham, Charles E., Company, 85

H

Hale, Barbara, 152, 164
Hays, Margaret, 123, 167-168, 178-189
Hood, C.I., Co., 16-17, 51-52, 114
Hood's Family, 16, 17, 51-52, 114, 130
Horsman, E. I., Company, 151, 152, 167

I

Ida Mae, McLoughlin Bros., 15, 22
Irene of Hesse, 125, 221, 235
Isabella of Spain, Queen, 221, 222, 224, 229

J

Jacobs, George W., and Company, 130, 146
Joan and her new Frocks, J. W. Spear Co., 90
Johnston, Annie Fellows, 75, 82
"Jointed Paper Doll Family," *The Woman's Magazine,* 130, 141-143
Journal des Petite Filles, 16, 24

K

Kaiserin und Prinzesschen, 124, 221, 224
Katie, Selchow and Righter, 63
"Kewpie Kutouts," *Woman's Home Companion,* 192, 193-200
Kewpies, 192-209
"Kewpies with Ragsy and Ritzy Cut-Out Dolls," Whitman Company, 122, 201-205
knickerbockers, 26, 27, 54
Kraemer, Gosta, 27

L

lace, 2

Ladies Home Journal, The, 3, 75, 130, 146-149, 167, 192
Ladies of the Sunday Art Supplement, 30-50
Ladies' World, 4
Lady Cyclists Up To Date, 16, 29
Lady Gay, McLoughlin Bros., 15, 21
"La Poupee Modele," 16, 24
Lee, Ella Dolbear, 144
Lettie Lane, Ladies' Home Journal, 3, 130, 146-149
"Lettie Lane Paper Family," 130, 146-149
Linson, Corwin Knapp, 4, 14, 84
Lion Coffee, 210, 211-218
  "Standing Brownies," 210, 211-214
  "Riding Brownies," 210, 215-218
"Little Colonel Series," 75, 82
Little Dolly Varden, McLoughlin Bros., 15, 24
"Little Dolly Varden" series, Mc-Loughlin Bros., 15, 24
Little Folks' Illustrated Annual 1913, 184-187
Little Folks' Annual 1915, 187-189
Little Folks Magazine, 167, 184-189
Little Kitty Cut-Up and Her Playmates, American Colortype, 158-159
Little Lady, McLoughlin Bros., 15, 21
Louise of Prussia, Queen, 221-222, 226

M
Madame Pompadour, McLoughlin Brothers, 222, 232
Maid of Honor, R. Tuck, 3, 6, 8, 112
Magazines
  Butterick, 75
  Canadian Home Journal, 190-191
  Delineator, The, 4, 14, 75, 84, 106, 130, 141, 144, 165, 192
  Designer, The, 106
  Farm and Home Magazine, 128
  Frank Leslie's Lady's Magazine, 16
  Godey's Lady's Book, 16
  Good Housekeeping, 4, 167, 192
  Journal des Petite Filles, 16, 24
  Ladies' Home Journal, The, 3, 75, 130, 146-149, 167, 192
  Ladies' World, 4,
  McCall's, 4, 130, 152, 164
  Pictorial Review, 4, 121, 130, 151, 152, 153, 167-177
  Woman's Home Companion, 4, 14, 192, 193-200
  Woman's Magazine, The, 130, 141, 152, 165
Mamie, Selchow and Righter, 63
Marchioness, McLoughlin Bros., 126, 222, 233
Margaret Butterick, The Delineator, 130, 144-145
Margherita of Italy, Queen, 222, 227, 231
Marie Antoinette of France, Queen; 221, 222, 225, 230
Marie Feodorovna, Czarina of Russia, 3, 222, 230
Marquis, McLoughlin Bros., 126, 222, 232-233
Mary, Queen of Scots, 222, 231
Mary Ware Doll Book, 75, 82-83
McCall's, 4, 130, 152, 164
"MC&K," 16, 50
McDonald, Margaret, 60
McLaughlin Coffee Company, 3, 9, 152, 222, 229-231
McLoughlin Brothers, 2, 4-5, 12, 15, 18-19, 20-24, 53, 54-56, 115, 116, 126, 151, 222, 232-233
  American Lady, 15, 20
  Betsy Brunette, 15, 23
  Bride, The, 2, 4
  Bride No. 0102, 12
  Bridegroom and Groomsman, 2, 5
  Bridesmaid, 2
  Clara West, 19
  Diane, the Bride, 3
  "Dolly Varden" series, 15, 23
  Ida Mae, 15, 22
  Lady Gay, 15, 21
  Little Dolly Varden, 15, 24
  "Little Dolly Varden" series, 15, 24
  Little Lady, 15, 21
  Madame Pompadour, 222, 232
  Marchioness, 126, 222, 233
  Marquis, 126, 222, 232-233
  Minnie Miller, 15, 22, 115

Mollie, 55
"Mulligan Guard Series," 232
Myra Mild, 54-55, 115, 116
"Paper Doll Bridal Party," 2, 4-5
Susie's Pets, 56, 116
Margery May's Big Sister, Woman's Home Companion, 14
"mechanical marionettes," 151, 155
Merry Marion, R. Tuck, 61
Miles, Dr., Medical Company, 70-71, 116
Miller, Mrs. Jenness, 26
Minard's Company, 86, 94-95
Minnie Miller, McLoughlin Bros., 15, 22, 115
Mollie, McLoughlin Bros., 55
Molly Cottontail, and Pa and Buster Bunny, McCall's Magazine, 164
Molly Munsing, Miss, 86, 108
Morgan, Wallace, 74, 80
"Mulligan Guard Series," McLoughlin Bros., 232
Munsingwear Company, 86, 108, 130, 140
Munsingwear Family, 130, 140
Musselman, M. Emma, 14
"My Book of Darling Dolls," Gabriel Co., 104-106
Myra Mild, McLoughlin Bros., 54-55, 115, 116
Myrtle Duck, Miss, 165

N
Napoleon III, 2
National Candy Company, 120, 151, 154
Nelson, O.W., Company, 86, 94-95
Nestle Company, 72
New York Biscuit Company, 210, 218
New York Herald, The, 74, 80
New York Mercury, 30
New York Sunday American, The, 130
Nicholas II, Czar of Russia, 222, 234
Noah's Ark Animals, R. Tuck, 151, 156-157
"Nursery Favorite Cut-Out Dolls," M. A. Donohue and Co., 180-181

O
Olive, Minard's, 95
O'Neill, Rose, 122, 192-209
Our Favorite Dolls, 64-67
Our Friends, the Bears, R. Tuck, 155
Our Little Treasure, R. Tuck, 3, 13, 112
Ottmann Litho Co., 74, 80, 151-152

P
"Paper Doll Bridal Party," McLoughlin Bros., 2, 4-5
Patriotic Dressing Dolls, American Colortype, 128-129
Peggy and her new Outfit, J. W. Spear Co., 89
Philadelphia Press, The, 30, 32, 167
Pictorial Review, 4, 121, 130, 151, 152, 153, 167-177
"Polly's Paper Playmates," 119, 130-139
Pompadour, Madame, 222, 232
Pope Manufacturing Co., 16, 26-28
Pretty Kitty, American Colortype, 121, 151, 158
Prima Donna Corsets, 30
Public Ledger, The, 130

R
Redfern, 26, 28
"Riding Brownies," Lion Coffee, 210, 215-218
"rockers," 151
Roosevelt, Teddy, 151, 154
Rosey Ruth, R. Tuck, 60
Ruffles, Fluffy, 74, 80

S
Saalfield Publishing Company
  "Scootles and Kewpie Doll Book," 122, 206-209
Saint Louis Republic, 30
Saint Nicholas, An Illustrated Magazine for Young Folks, 167, 210
Sallie, Peter Thomson Co., 57
San Francisco Chronicle, The, 30
Scootles, 122, 192, 206-209
"Scootles and Kewpie Doll Book," Saalfield Ca., 122, 206-209
"Seesaws," 151, 156
Selchow and Righter, 53, 63, 64-66, 120, 151-152

Flossie, 63
Katie, 63
Mamie, 63
Our Favorite Dolls, 64-66
Teddy Bear Paper Doll, 120, 151-152
Singer Sewing Machine Company, 3, 9
Spear, J.W., Company, 54, 86-90, 119
  Daisy and her Dresses, 88
  Joan and her new Frocks, 90
  Peggy and her new Outfit, 89
  Spear's Original Character Dolls, 86
Spear's Original Character Dolls, 86
"Standing Brownies," Lion Coffee, 210, 211-214
Stecher Company of Rochester, 85
Stokes Publishing Company, 126, 221, 224-228
Sunday Sun, The, 74, 75
Susan, Gabriel Co., 101
Susie's Pets, McLoughlin Bros., 56, 116
Sweet Alice, R. Tuck, 61-62
Sylvia and Her Seven Frocks, The Designer, 106

T
Teddy Bear, Selchow and Righter, 120, 151-152
Teddy Bear, 151
Ted E. Bear Goes A-Hunting, Pictorial Review, 151, 153
Tommy Atkins on Furlough, The Delineator, 4, 14
Thompson, Charles, Company, 85
Thomson, Peter, Co., 53, 57
  Sallie, 57
Three Little Kittens, The, R. Tuck, 155
trousseau, 2, 6
Tuck, Raphael, Co., 3, 6-8, 13, 53, 54, 60-62, 74, 81, 86, 112, 151, 155, 156-157
  "Artistic Toy Novelty Series," 151
  "Bridal Party Series of Dressing Dolls," 3, 6-8, 112
  Bride and Her Trousseau, The, 3, 6, 112
  Bridegroom, The, 6, 7, 112
  Dear Dorothy, 60
  "Dolls For All Seasons," 60-61
  Fanny Fairleigh, 74, 81
  Father Tuck's Doll Sheets, 6
  Father Tuck's Marionettes, 155
  Merry Marion, 61
  Noah's Ark Animals, 151, 156-157
  Our Little Treasure, 3, 13, 112
  Rosey Ruth, 60
  Sweet Alice, 61-62
Tucker, E. S., 126, 224
"Turkish pants," 16

U
Universal Toy Company, 12

V
Varden, Dolly, 15-16
Victoria of England, Queen, 2, 15, 221, 222, 227, 228
Victoria of Sweden, Crown Princess, 222, 230

W
Washington, Martha, 16, 221, 222, 226, 231
Washington Star, The, 30
Weidersiem, Grace, 167
Whitman Company, 122, 130, 201-205
  "Kewpies with Ragsy and Ritzy Cut-Out Dolls," 122, 201-205
Wilhelm II of Prussia, Kaiser, 125, 221, 235
Wilken, Eloise Burns, 104
Willis, Bess Goe, 165
Winkle Family, The, Gabriel Co., 130, 150
Woolson Spice Company, 211
Woolworth, F.W., Company, 85, 91-92
Woman's Home Companion, 4, 14, 192, 193-200
Woman's Magazine, The, 130, 141, 152, 165
Worth, Charles Frederick, 2

Y
Young, Sheila, 3, 130, 146

Z
"Zouave trousers," 16, 28